BLEEDING
MOUNTAINS
OF NEPAL

ADITYA MAN SHRESTHA

EKTA BOOKS
Kathmandu, Nepal

First Published in 1999 by *Ekta Books*
Reprinted 2000

Distribution Information: *Ekta Books Distributors Pvt. Ltd.*
GPO Box: 6445, Thapathali, Kathmandu, Nepal
Tel: 977-1-260482, 260014, 260083; Fax: 977-1-260744
E-mail: ektabook@mos.com.np

ISBN 99933-1-902-3

Artwork: *Kishor Joshi*
Computer: *S.K. Dongol*

Printed in Nepal for *Ekta Books*,
at *Monaj Offset Press Pvt. Ltd.*, Kathmandu

*Dedicated to the poor
and exploited*

Contents

PART IV
Industry, Commerce and Exploitation

PART V
Irrigation, Electricity and Illusions

PART VI
Aid, Advice and Miscarriage

Preface

I would like to remember at this moment Mr Bhuwaneshor Khatri, a close friend of mine, who familiarised me during our common assignment in the royal palace of Nepal in the seventies with the world of power misuse for personal gain. In fact, he inspired me to write an account of such episodes that would open the lid on the secrets of amassing wealth. He was throughout his life a civil servant, an honest one at that, but he had a sharp tongue which earned him more enemies than friends. But King Birendra of Nepal understood his spirit, admired him and as a token of his appreciation nominated him as Nepal's governing representative to the Asian Development Bank. Unfortunately, he died before I could venture into this project which I admit with all humility was a brainchild of his. Better late than never. I pray for peace to his departed soul.

It was my association with Transparency International Nepal in 1997 that inspired me to produce this collection. It was association with its eminent members, especially Dr Devendra Raj Panday, that provided me an insight into many issues related to misuse of state power and financial misappropriation.

This enterprise was however made possible within a relatively short period of time by the co-operation of Mr Rajendra Dahal, a rising Nepali journalist, who is highly knowledgeable about the water resources of Nepal.

There are numerous people who have helped me in gathering information, explaining them and unravelling various complex issues to me. I would like to thank the following for their sincere help in this respect: Prof. Surendra Bahadur Shrestha, Mr Madhav Ghimire, Mr Bishwoman Shrestha, Mr Anil Chitrakar, Mr Ramesh Dhungel, Mr Mohan Mainali, Mr Bihari Krishna Shrestha, Mr Prakash C. Joshi, Mr Ishor Onta and, last but not least, Mr Bishnu Bahadur KC, the Auditor General of Nepal.

Mr Bhairab Risal deserves special thanks from me for helping in information collection and public relations. I must also thank Mr Ram Pradhan who was kind enough to do a painstaking job of revising the manuscript and improving the overall texture of presentation. Mr Druzhba Maharjan and Mr Sarun Tuladhar have also been of immense assistance in completing this work. I am equally indebted to Mr Hem Bahadur Bista for his constant support from start to finish.

There are a few others who would not like to be named in this book. However I would like to recognise their contributions. Lastly, I feel gratified with my family members for standing by me in this endeavour throughout.

The information has been derived mostly from published materials and the rest has come from authentic sources. However, interpretations are solely mine and I hold full responsibility for any discrepancy thereof.

I have used the original dollar figures wherever available. When not available, an equivalent conversion of the Nepalese rupees has been used more for conceptual clarity than precision. I have avoided its use wherever I felt it not essential for explaining the issues in question.

My utmost effort throughout has been to stress simplicity and clarity rather than mathematical exactitude. I hope my readers will let me off with sympathetic understanding.

Thanks for holding it in your hand.

– **Aditya Man Shrestha**
Kathmandu, 1999

Prologue

The world knows Nepal by its array of the highest mountains on earth. Millions of tourists have seen the glory and grandeur of these peaks. But the world is yet to know Nepal's inside story, particularly how these natural beauties are bled by internal and external predators. It is a story of corruption, greed, misuse of power and resources inside Nepal and the pain inflicted on it from outside. Will not these deplorable phenomena leave this country of 20 million people perennially impoverished, ignorant and miserable? *Bleeding Mountains of Nepal is* a close-up narrative of the mishmash of the developments in the last fifty years - the tears behind the smiles.

Nepal, a small happy country on the lap of the great Himalayas, was forced to open to the world in 1951 by revolution. Over half a century of mingling and interaction with the modern world later, this idyllic abode of peace is today a restless and discontented society. The glories of the past, be it bravery in the battlefield or gallantry at home or honesty everywhere has slowly been overshadowed by an abject image of poverty, corruptibility and unreliability. Such a projection is inspired by the fact that Nepalese society is today managed and run by a bunch of people whose greed, avarice and unabashed dereliction of public duty is best left unsaid. The politician is never tired of professing dedication to the people's welfare but pursues only his own narrow, parochial interest. He seeks the people's mandate to rule the country and, once in power, engages in minting money. A civil servant takes oath to serve the people whom he actually loathes. He thinks he is paid to while away his time in the office and works only when he is assured of extra benefits.

A businessman is not satisfied with a fair margin of profit and resorts to unfair means to amass wealth. An industrialist does not believe in the development of his enterprise in real terms but uses it to make fast bucks by hoodwinking the consumers and the banks into financing bogus ventures. Farmers take loans for farm inputs and to boost production, but spend the money on the weddings of their wards. The university teachers get monthly pay for no work but when they really work they get overtime. The doctors go to the government hospitals only to catch new clients for their private clinics.

The low morale in the public offices can to a large extent be traced to Nepal's long history of power misuse for personal gain. Throughout the recorded history of Nepal, she has been ruled by kings. The divine right theory reigned supreme, insisting that the country and the people are the king's personal property. The kings of Nepal gave away land to their courtiers as a token of appreciation for their loyal services. Nothing rankled as long as the land accommodated the royal wish. But with population growth and development the land for free distribution got smaller. Land donation then in the latter half of the twentieth century began to be looked down upon as an abuse of authority and misuse of national resources. Estimates are that one third of Nepal's territory had been doled out to those who were adept in pleasing the reigning monarchs.

For one hundred years, from the mid-nineteenth century to the mid-twentieth century, Nepal was ruled by one large family of the Ranas. They had a free hand in seizing as much land as they wished. The big palaces standing today in Kathmandu valley adorned with French windows, gigantic gardens and tall brick walls were all built during this period. After the Rana's downfall in 1951, the Shah kings took charge but the practice of land grabbing and land donation to palace favourites remained as it was. King Mahendra stood out as a great giver of public land and forest to his henchmen. When he came face to face with violent political opposition in 1962, two years after the dismissal of a popularly elected government, he bought political loyalty from a goodly number of people to prop up his regime. He indeed succeeded in his royal mission but it cost the country dearly.

In 1972, when King Birendra ascended the throne on the sudden death of his shrewd father, the transfer of power was peaceful and orderly and perhaps for the first time in history no palace coups or political conspiracies threatened to disrupt the succession process. The young monarch inherited, unlike his predecessors, an undisputed kingship and an entrenched political system called the Panchayat, with some democratic trappings, a fairly wide international relationships and a palace pyramid with a strong grip over the administration. Having been exposed to liberal education in England, Japan and the United States, it was widely believed that he had the requisite qualifications to take over the reins of command and leadership of his country.

The new King, full of aplomb and ideas, started his rule literally with a bang. He called in some bright and dynamic people to his palace and assigned them the task of looking into different sectors of public life and national development, and to recommend measures to set right the wrongs. It was indeed a bold experiment that raised eyebrows in the traditional power pockets of Nepal. No less unnerved were the privileged class who thrived on palace favours. The nobility was indeed afraid when the King started scratching the wealth amassed through corrupt practices.

The King began with his own house. He ordered an investigation into the privileges the members of the royal family had received in commerce and industry. Although the report never saw the light of day, it was difficult to hide the facts as they were more or less known to the public. Big hotels, big travel agencies and big industries were either owned or controlled by the royal family, so much so that international trade was running under its direct patronage. Royal family members could bring planeloads of foreign liquor for their hotels without paying the duty, whereas ordinary people were charged up to 200% import duty on such commodities. The royals had free access to the hard currency reserve of the country but stringent regulations were imposed on the common people who were allowed only $200 to $500 for foreign travel.

If the King could bring his close relatives to book it was a clear signal that he would not spare anyone, however high his or her position may be in the official hierarchy. He made a quick move by ordering an independent probe into alleged misuse of power, public finance and national resources. Consequently, he pulled up the defaulters and sacked the wrongdoers, but he did not forget to reward those who were honest. The whole administration was shaken by the young King's determination to cleanse the bureaucracy. High-level corruption touched an all-time low.

But the situation was not sustained for long. Hardly a year had passed when the King, sometime in 1973, was brought under tremendous pressure to relax his assault on the misuse of authority and corrupt practices. As the years wore on, the Queen, initially behind the curtains, came in front to manage public funds through social organisations which were encouraged to proliferate. The irony is that the ordinary citizens were debarred from establishing even innocuous associations like the Geological Society of Nepal.

All the princes and princesses headed different national and international organisations based in Nepal. Not a single leaf would move without one or another member of the royal family nodding his or her approval. The King stood as a helpless spectator. Public ire went on piling up against the royal excesses until it finally burst in the form of the people's movement in 1990.

Unfortunately, the radical political change failed to bring about a commensurate change in the make-hay-while-the-sun-shines scenario. The Ranas who iron-handedly ruled Nepal for over a century till 1950 were criticised for personalising the national treasury. One of the Rana prime ministers, who managed the country for twenty-eight years, is believed to have deposited Rs. 90 million in the names of each of his nine sons in foreign banks. At that time, no national budgetary system was in place. A public accounting system was introduced later but the misuse of public money never ended.

All through the thirty-year direct rule of the King, from 1960 to 1990, corruption flourished with impunity as the pattern of development issues involving public money became more and more complex. Even the great anti-royalist uprising of 1990 could not redress this problem despite the promises made by the political leaders. Under the parliamentary dispensation, which replaced the Panchayat system, corruption continues unabated. Ironically, it is too transparent, too rampant.

In this historical perspective, the Nepalese people have perceived state power as an instrument for self aggrandisement, wealth and social status. In no way can this impression be dispelled as those who became millionaires overnight were left alone by all governments to savour their loot. The ugly truth is most of the people in the top ten per cent bracket today achieved affluence through dubious deals.

Under Nepalese rules, no bank can question the source of the money deposited with it. The tax authorities can deal only with the visible incomes of individuals. The anticorruption agency can prosecute people found guilty of misusing power but the sudden spurt of wealth in the hands of an individual does not come within its purview as it can easily be disguised as 'my wife's dowry'. So, no matter what it is oligarchy, monarchy or democracy - the state, to all intents and purposes, is a goose that lays the golden eggs.

Foreigners are, however, not far behind the natives in fleecing this poor country as much as possible by marketing Nepal's poverty and backwardness. The World Bank and the Asian Development Bank want to push loans for good or bad purposes. The donor countries pretend to give a big free gift but keep the major part to themselves. The expatriate experts excel in promoting their own interests, the advisers proffer advice which never works, the consultants are good in hiking up their consultancy fees. It Is this cumulative ganging-up that causes the Nepalese poor to bleed in pain and moan in despair.

◆

PART I
Exposure, Experience and Insight

Chapter One

The First Encounter

As an officer on special duty at the royal palace of Nepal for two years in 1973 and 1974, I had a rare opportunity to see the top decision makers of Nepal. It was the time when the King was in supreme command of state affairs under a constitution that vested sovereign power in the monarchy and the political system ran under his direct leadership. King Birendra inherited the whole system from his father and wanted to give a personal twist to bring it closer to the people. Besides treading a non-traditional path of hiring highly educated and relatively young advisers in the palace, he created a new wing for brainstorming, in-depth studies and investigation, drafting new development plans and programmes. I was in one of the groups that were put together for these purposes.

It was during this crucial period that I was put in a team to probe corruption cases. It was a new exposure and education for me as I had no personal experience in government administration. Thanks to other members of the team, who were veterans in administrative and financial affairs, I could get a closer view of how decisions were manipulated to serve the personal interests of the officials.

There was, for example, one alleged case of corruption in the Department of Food Research. It had the approved programmes and budget to conduct food research and in that connection procured equipment from a foreign country. But the machinery was meant for large-scale food packaging, not useful for research. But the director of the department defended the import on the plea that he planned to produce cheap processed food for mass consumption in Nepal. He expressed great concern for the poor and the starving people of Nepal and argued that the machine would help feed them at a low cost. He was very eloquent in his defence.

There was, however, a clear flaw in his action. The machine was supplied by an agency owned by his wife. There was nothing legally wrong as his wife had a right to do business. It was also revealed that the director acted as a consultant to the company. That too was in order as far as the government regulations were concerned. The government officials were allowed to act as technical consultants to private agencies for a fee. So in terms of technicalities, the director could not be legally prosecuted.

However, his motive was more than clear. He put in an order for such a big machine as it yielded a higher commission to the supplier agency which belonged to none other than his wife. The amount was enough to build a house in Nepal. The director was nonetheless sacked from his job without being charged, as the evidence was not considered adequate to prosecute him in a court of law. The machinery was put into operation only once but left to rust over time as the government had no policy to mass produce food of this kind.

The same agency, in another case under investigation, had obtained a government licence for a food-processing industry in Nepal. To start with, it planned to install a dairy factory to supply fresh and pasteurised milk to the people in the capital city. As there was no cattle farming in the valley for a regular supply of milk, the factory sought the permission of the government to import condensed milk as a 'raw material'. It looked fair enough on the surface.

But the commerce department which issued the licence for import had some reservations. Before issuing a permit, the department wanted to be sure that the dairy factory was really being built. It enquired if the necessary land had been purchased, buildings erected and equipment procured. The licence could produce no evidence of any moves he had made to set up the factory. So initially he was refused the import permit. However, after waiting for a few months, when the objecting officials were absent he managed to have the licence issued. The demand for condensed milk in the local market was high, which meant he could make good money without taking the pains to process it. When the case was investigated, the flaws came to the surface. Officials who were responsible for the decision were penalised and those who had objected to it were rewarded. The permit was consequently cancelled.

◆

Chapter Two

No Room For Honesty

I got further insight into the official decision-making process when I was an adviser to the Minister for Information and Communication of Nepal. The honorary job lasted for three months, from July to September of 1997, under a left-right coalition government of the UML (United Marxists-Leninists) and RPP (Rashtriya Prajatantra Party).

Pre-appointment discussion with the Minister concerned revealed that there was no budgetary provision in his ministry to pay an adviser. Besides, the cabinet had already put a moratorium on the appointment of advisers on grounds of austerity. The only option, as it were, was to make a public-sector organisation under the jurisdiction of the ministry bear the burden. As it would take considerable time to process the idea and the Minister wanted my services as soon as possible, I agreed to serve without a salary.

But this simple fact was not understood when the government announced my appointment. The newscast mentioned the honorary nature of the appointment, triggering a series of speculations based on individual perceptions.

The comments I received from my personal as well as professional friends on the honorary nature of the assignment were as unfair as they were unjustified. Contrary to my expectations, the reactions smacked more of deprecation than appreciation.

If I were to put their feelings in a nutshell I would say that my honorary service to the government was regarded as a mysterious and incomprehensible acquiescence. This can be attributed to the common perception in Nepal that a government position is a vending machine for power and privileges. An honorary job simply does not fit into this kind of popular perception and hence is untenable.

Some went a step further in their suspicion that I was taking unseen and, therefore, unfair benefits out of my assignment. Otherwise, in their own view, there was no reason why I should work free when the Minister himself was drawing a full salary and enjoying all the perks from the government. I can hardly dispute their logic. But the truth of the matter was that there were absolutely no material benefits accruing to me except the satisfaction I was drawing from the job. I defended myself on the ground that since I enjoyed the job of advising the Minister on matters of importance to do with mass communication, I did not mind working free for the government.

But in a country where the success of a man is measured by how much wealth he is able to amass irrespective of the means, it was useless to try to justify my voluntary service to the government. On the contrary, people take pride in showing off their wealth by putting up multi-storeyed buildings without proper planning and without paying any attention to the aesthetic aspect of the architecture. The popular perception of moneymaking does not leave any room for appreciation of a selfless, voluntary service to the government.

However, the assignment did not go unrewarded. The interactions I had during the period with the bureaucracy and people in general proved very valuable in understanding the secrets of power that normally drive people out of their minds, and how power is misused. The first thing people expected from me as I joined office was the sanctioning of a telephone line from the Minister. The distribution of telephone lines being restricted, getting a line sanctioned without going through the usual red tape is a great privilege that people known to me wanted from me. Nobody cared or discussed with me how I could help the government reorientate its communication priorities.

This has led me to believe that those in power have been denigrated and diminished in the eyes of the people. They are too weak to help alleviate the impoverished masses of Nepal. I came out with no doubt in my mind that my services have been completely misunderstood in the broader national context of a power game in which there is obviously no place for honesty.

◆

Chapter Three

Unfulfilled Promises

I knew the Ministry of Information and Communication was a very inefficient ministry. Were it not so, there would be no need for an extraneous help from advisers like me. Apart from the ministry's inability to deal with matters of national importance, a few small instances of unfulfilled promises reinforced this general impression. Circumstances surrounding my appointment letter, office space and transport were rather amusing.

It took several weeks for an appointment letter to be drafted after the Minister had approved the idea of making me his adviser. Several weeks passed before the letter was delivered to me. It took yet another couple of weeks before the ministry gave me an office to operate from. A small room on the Minister's floor was vacated in my favour but the officials previously occupying the place moved all the furniture away to their new office.

It was quite interesting to find that everybody from the Secretary down to other functionaries took it for granted that the room was already allotted to me and I was comfortably seated there. It is very typical of our bureaucrats to assume things are done once they make a decision, irrespective of what happens and of the fact that the reality may be entirely different. But when they came to know that it had not yet been done, their reaction was subdued. Invariably, they blame others and the others blame yet another set of others. I could never identify who could get it done as planned. So, I stopped raising this issue and started operating from my own private office in Tripureshwor which is just five minutes' drive from the ministry complex in Singh Durbar.

To my surprise, one day I found my name plate hanging on the wall opposite the Minister's office. Out of sheer curiosity - not pleasure - I peeped in to see what kind of room had finally been allocated to me. There were two small desks and a few chairs. A number of visitors had already crowded around the personal assistant to the Minister. My supposed seat was unoccupied but the table was surrounded by the visitors. Nobody except the PA recognised me. He invited me to take my seat. He then resumed conversation with the visitors, one of whom was using the telephone on my desk; everybody was talking with everybody. After a few minutes, when I could no longer stand the noise, I walked out.

I found one official in the next room who always locked himself in. On my enquiry, he told me that I would soon understand why he had to do it. He was dead right as I understood why within the next few days.

One afternoon, I was in my room browsing through some official papers. The door was wide open and the visitors in the corridor were peeping in and out. As their loud conversation disturbed my concentration, I decided to shut the door but to my disgust every two minutes somebody would open the door, look in and go. It was simply a nuisance. Some intrepid visitors walked in without permission, lifted the telephone and started dialling.

Some of them took the chairs to start conversations, completely disregarding my presence. This led me to lock the door from the inside. But that did not help as knocks were monotonously repetitious. This with thumping of shoes on the corridor and loud conversations not only drove me crazy but drove me out of the building. Since then I dared not use the room for any serious business.

The only facility the government had promised me in return for my voluntary services was a vehicle. Although I had my own means of transport I was not in a position to drive it regularly due to a back pain. The Minister was under the impression that since he had endorsed the idea of providing a vehicle for me I already had one. The Secretary who was supposed to authorise it was not confident that he could ever do it but he never confessed his inability to the Minister. There were two options open to him.

One was to requisition a vehicle from the central pool and the second was to pull one up from a government-owned corporation.

It turned out that the central pool was itself under great pressure since the ministers and members of parliament heading different legislative or administrative committees tended never to return government vehicles in their possession even when they were out of office. Only extraordinary pressure from the ministry could fish out a vehicle from the pool. Either the Secretary was incapable of doing it or not willing to do so. In any case nothing worked from that sector.

The other possibility was a public organisation. The only agency which could supply an extra vehicle for the ministry's use was the Nepal Telecommunication Corporation (NTC). Its chairman, obviously to pre-empt the issue, never missed an opportunity to complain that the ministry was already using eight of his vehicles, three of them by the Minister himself

In that situation, I believed neither the Minister nor the Secretary had the moral strength to ask the corporation chief to supply an additional vehicle for my use. So, I stayed silent on this subject till I held the honorary job. I felt kind of relieved when the left-right combine collapsed. The Minister was out, so was I of the adviser's responsibility.

◆

Chapter Four

A Shabby Track Record

If one were to take the Ministry of Information and Communication as representative of the government system in Nepal, I must say the bureaucracy stands as a major hindrance to progress. Its shabby performance is a blot on the history of public administration in Nepal. The civil service gained its importance when the select band of educated people joined it after the downfall of the Rana regime which revelled in hiring and firing government officials once a year at the whims and fancy of the presiding autocrat. In the fifty year history of permanent civil service, modelled on the Western system, the Nepalese bureaucrats developed a high public profile equal to or greater than that of the political figures. The news of appointment, transfer and dismissal of senior civil servants always made bigger headlines than would the news concerning the politicians.

For over thirty years of the King's direct rule in Nepal, from 1960 to 1990, it was the civil servants who actually governed the country, not the ministers who were nevertheless held politically accountable. Padma Bahadur Khatri, Yadunath Khanal, Bishnumani Acharya and Kulshekhar Sharma are some of the stalwarts in public administration who dominated the administrative firmament of their times much more than their ministerial bosses, including the prime minister. It is all because they derived their power directly from the King who was everything in those days. Civil servants who were known for their honesty, integrity and competence were few and they have left their office.

The inception of a parliamentary democracy in Nepal in 1990 sadly struck just too many blows to the so-called permanent civil service. The bulk of the senior civil servants was pruned out in 1993 in a drastic action of the government. Besides creating an utter sense of instability in public administration, the action created an administrative vacuum, not only in terms of power exercise but also in terms of competence in decision-making. With the change of hands from one party to another, from the Congress to the Communists and again from the Communists to the Congress and from the Congress to a coalition, the bureaucrats - especially at the top level - were shunted as if they were security guards at public institutions.

The Ministry of Information and Communication presents a far worse case. It is manned by officials who have no competence whatsoever in modem communication systems. As they have no education or training background in communication, for them to take any initiative in developing the communication sector is out of the question. The officials, who have been there for many years, are there just to move the files. They usually don't know what they are talking about. But by virtue of their being in the ministry for such and such number of years they don't hesitate in claiming expertise which they never have had. There is no doubt, though, about their ability to shoot down innovative ideas, especially when it comes from an 'outsider' like me.

The ministry has the lowest level of co-ordination among high officials. Outwardly many of them welcomed me but I could feel that at heart they were resentful.

Individually they sought my help in raising important issues that they were handling before the Minister. Officials below the Secretary have no direct access to the Minister. The Secretary would allow his subordinates to see the Minister only on matters in which he wanted to pass the buck over to somebody else. The joint secretaries and the undersecretaries who were in charge of administration, information, technical matters, etc. were acting as autonomous entities. They found fault with every other person in the ministry except themselves. They made it appear as if they were the only ones who were sincere, efficient and dependable - which of course they were certainly not.

To inform the Minister only partly and in a highly biased and exaggerated form was SOP (standard operational procedure) in the ministry. Based on his own experience, the Minister did not believe the officials. The officials presented their files at the eleventh hour, allowing the Minister virtually no time to think the matter over. Expediency and urgency would press upon the Minister to sign off the files irrespective of his doubts about the integrity of the officials. In the worst cases, the officials would conceal the files, pluck out important papers and tamper with information to hoodwink the Minister into decisions favourable to them in one way or another. I found some cases of such tampering and brought them to the notice of the Minister who was, to my surprise, not surprised. He said he was not unaware of such things happening. He knew from his earlier stint in the government.

The only area that was handled promptly and seriously was the opportunity to travel abroad. The ministry is flooded with invitations to international training programmes, seminars, workshops and conferences. The officials first try to keep away from their colleagues and prepare the files in such a way that it is only himself or herself who deserves to be nominated for participation. Such files are never delayed; rather they are followed up with great devotion. He or she pleads as if the whole nation could fall apart should somebody else get the ministerial nod.

The net result is the important decisions get delayed or prove faulty, generating unpopular public reaction suspicious of corruption. Small wonder that this ministry has a poor track record, and an even poorer public image of itself. In the final count, it is the country which reels under the weight of inefficiency in public administration.

◆

Chapter Five

Locked and Keyed

When a man becomes a minister in Nepal, overnight he is transformed into a demi-god. He is surrounded by a sea of visitors at home as well as in the office. For all practical purposes, he loses his privacy and becomes a 'public man' in the negative sense of the term.

The day I met my minister it was an unusual day for me but something very routine for him. It was a Saturday, the only day the government offices remain closed. It is the traditional R and R weekend. But for the Minister it is business as usual, a regular day full of appointments, public commitments and meetings.

Since he had some problems with his ligaments the doctors had advised bed rest for a few days. However, he could operate from his home and was in fact holding all meetings in his bedroom. When I reached there, the living room was overflowing with people. Some visitors were standing and moving to and fro in the room and entreating the Private Secretary to let them have the *darshan* of the Minister as soon as possible. But with droves of grievances up their sleeves, they were not sure if they would ever be able to see the Minister and, if so, when?

I had no problem in meeting the Minister although it was an hour later than agreed upon. The Secretary was with the Minister on some official business. By the time I got out of his home it was already twelve noon and half of the visiting band was gone without the much sought after *darshan*. On the one hand, I pitied them because they had wasted time and energy in waiting. On the other, I was not sure if it was proper to visit a minister on an officially free day, unless called upon on prior appointments.

Evening time was no better. Once I was at his home around 9 p.m. for some urgent consultation. That was when he was expected back from a cultural engagement. But when he got back it was already 10 p.m. Since there already was a crowd of members of parliament, I was asked to wait *sine die*. He hardly took five minutes to change into casual wear. I saw him briefly around 11 p.m. By that time I was too tired to hold any stimulating conversation with him. His visitors were still around and I later learnt that he was left alone only after midnight.

In fact, the office was even worse as far as the crowding was concerned. Technically, public visitors are allowed only after 3 p.m. But no minister can observe it strictly. So his visitors' room is always brimming with people, delegations from the villages, job seekers, party workers, journalists, foreign visitors, and last but not the least, new telephone line hunters.

It is an established fact of Nepal that the telephone distribution tragically takes 90% of the time of the Minister for Information and Communication. Normally the distribution of telephones is not his responsibility, but the severe scarcity of lines drags him into this unsavoury work. There are at present about one hundred thousand telephone lines whereas the demand is at least two times more. Those who adhere to due process ruled by the Nepal Telecommunication Corporation have to wait for five to ten years. The lines are also made available if somebody is prepared to pay five times more than the normal charge.

The only option left is the Minister's recommendation. One pays the normal charge and starts calling up people sooner than the rest.

One afternoon, I was called by the Minister to his office. I rushed from my private office at Tripureshwor to the ministry to find the whole passage to the Minister's chamber full of people. When the Private Secretary noticed me in the crowd, he had a hard time approaching me. When both of us tried to get into the Minister's chamber hustling through the crowd of telephone or job seekers we found the room locked. After a knock, the gateman half-opened the door to check who had knocked. He immediately locked the door once we were in.

It was only the antechamber we had got in to. The small room just outside the Minister's room was also filled with visitors who had had their appointments already fixed. Since there was no seating arrangement everybody was standing in suspense. We too had to wait because the Minister's room too was bolted from inside. We knocked and after several minutes the door opened and we were let In.

The Minister's chamber was no better. There was a crowd here too. And the Minister was nowhere to be seen. He was in his private chamber just adjacent to the big room. Obviously, he had prioritised his visitors. He came out of the private chamber followed by five persons and no sooner had he sat down on his chair, than he was surrounded by people who were already there in the room. He was listening to this man, shaking hands with the other and receiving petition papers from yet another. He was speaking to somebody, gesturing to the other with his eyes and hands which were moving all over, all around.

I was seated in one corner, watching a virtual pandemonium at the Minister's desk. He somehow managed to patiently dispose of them. When he was about to speak about the urgent issue in question with me, a group of visitors crashed in. The group was led by a powerful and aggressive member of parliament and no one had the courage to stop him. It was again a request for a telephone line in his constituency, which the Minister immediately granted by signing the application. The MP then started some conversation with the Minister, that had no relevance whatsoever to his visit nor to any matter of importance. The Minister looked relieved to see him go, followed by the group he had barged in with.

It was already past office time and since the Minister had to rush to another meeting I came back without any discussion with him. I was wondering if this was the proper way a minister should function. Finally, fed-up with the pestering crowd with telephone demands, he delegated all his 'telephone' power to his deputy, the Minister of State for Information and Communication. The venue for the milling crowd changed but it remained undiminished, thanks to the unresolved scarcity of telephone lines in the country.

◆

PART II
Power, Misuse and Benefits

Chapter Six

Too Many, Too Expensive

Nepal is a small country of twenty million people. But the number of ministers appointed to govern it is often unmanageably big. At one time in 1995 it climbed to forty-eight, giving it the dubious title of a jumbo cabinet. The bloated size of the government has been the direct fallout of the compulsion of forming coalition governments in Nepal from 1993 to 1997. To keep the government going, the prime ministers took everyone worth the name from smaller coalescing political parties as a minister irrespective of his credentials. In the course of government-making, six governments have come into being in the name of stability in the same number of years. Intense horse-trading for ministerial berths has become a common feature and, despite promises to the contrary, the size of the cabinet has not shrunk no matter which combination of parties is in power.

In such a large cabinet, the prime minister always faces a severe problem in allocating portfolios to the ministers. For want of adequate number of ministries, the prime minister ends up creating new ministries by dismembering the existing ones. The number has now unjustifiably swelled to thirty-six ministries. The other option is to maintain several ministers without portfolio who operate from their own homes because they have no office.

Be that as it may, the ministers are entitled to certain privileges and perks. A minister of any rank is paid Rs. 62,000 (about $1,000) per month. The sum includes his salary, residence telephone, house rent and utilities, fuel, and residence hospitality. In addition, about Rs. 100,000 is taken out of the national exchequer per month to cover the cost of his private office, official vehicles, newspapers, office hospitality, travel, security guards and communications. Altogether, a Minister costs the country more than Rs. 160,000 per month.

Accordingly, for forty-eight ministers, this regular expense comes to Rs. 7,680,000 per month; in annual terms it comes to Rs. 92,160,000. The amount does not include the ministers' foreign travels. Though from the standpoint of the volume of work and the size of the country, smaller cabinets make sense, political expediency imposes such a heavy - and totally avoidable - burden on the taxpayers.

The use of national resources on unproductive political grounds can never be justified when one takes into consideration the pathetic plight of the poor people in Nepal. According to an estimate, one Minister's expense if diverted can save ten thousand Nepalese mothers from tetanus deaths every month in a country where 55% of neonatal deaths are caused by tetanus in the rural areas. There has actually been a 75% reduction in tetanus-related deaths under a government programme but the only visible reason why it could not be fully effective is the lack of resources which of course are shamelessly squandered in sustaining the elephantine cabinet.

Similarly, one Minister's expenses can save twenty-five thousand Nepalese children from dying by dehydration in a country where diarrhoea is by far the biggest killer, taking a toll of forty-five thousand children every year. In the same way, one Minister's pay and perks is sufficient to supply iodised salt to 10,500 people suffering from physical and mental deformities. The mountain people particularly suffer from goitre and other deformities because they do not get iodised salt at an affordable price.

Similarly, about fifteen thousand people can be freed from parasitic diseases with expenses incurred by a Minister in one month. It can also be used for the supply of vitamin A to about thirty thousand children who suffer from night blindness. It is also enough to build thirty-seven toilets in rural schools with no such facility. It can be adequate to supply safe drinking water to four schools. Almost 7,500 pneumonia cases can be cured. In a country reeling under abject poverty and deprivation, the real problems of the people are always just too many and too serious. Instead of addressing the problems with the available resources, far too many ministers are being maintained for no good reason. ◆

Chapter Seven

Arbitrary Diversions

The Office of the Auditor General of Nepal, a statutory body that examines the propriety of the use of public funds, comes out annually with two voluminous reports containing its findings and comments on the income and expenditure of all the government departments and the state-owned agencies. The reports make serious but at times amusing reading. The reports of 1997 contain a long list of revealing instances as to how the public-utility fund allocated for medical services to the poor people was diverted to 'the personal health' of the health ministers. No wonder the sick continue to suffer while the ministers are smiling.

The following list is an authentic enumeration and explanation of the misuse of public funds:

1. Rs. 293,000 was diverted from the programme on family planning and maternity and child care to repair and maintain the vehicle of the health minister. The minister is provided a separate fund for this purpose from the regular budget.

2. Rs. 18,000 was used from the regular budget of the Health Department to pay for the travel of the minister's personal staff.

3. Rs. 2,400,000 was spent for the maintenance of the minister's vehicle from the leprosy-control programme. No minister needs so much money for vehicle maintenance.

4. Rs. 4,000 was given to the Minister for his car fuel from the budget of the Health Department. The Minister gets regular fuel expenses from the government.

5. Rs. 280,000 belonging to a programme for supply of medical equipment to the ill-equipped hospitals and health posts was used to repair and maintain the minister's vehicles.

6. Rs. 68,000 appropriated for a programme to supply medicines to the village health posts was used for the repair and maintenance of a state health minister's vehicle.

7. Rs. 409,000 belonging to the medical-equipment supply programme was used to refurbish the health minister's office.

8. The programme on medical-equipment supply to the hospitals also paid Rs. 75,000 to buy the cassette recorder and newspapers for the minister who gets a regular allowance for these items.

9. Rs. 20,000 was paid from the Health Department's regular budget for the minister's travel allowance, fuel and stationery and cassettes acquired by him. The allowances for these purposes are drawn by the minister separately.

10. Rs. 37,000 was paid to the assistant health minister for vehicle repair and maintenance from the budget of the national health education and information programme.

11. Rs. 23,000 was illegally paid to him for the same purpose from the budget of a programme for AIDS and other sexually transmitted diseases control.

12. Rs. 29,000 was paid to him again for the same purpose from the tuberculosis control programme.

13. Rs. 75,000 was paid for buying a cassette recorder and newspaper subscriptions for the assistant health minister from the budget of medical equipment supply programme.

14. Rs. 21,000 was paid from the regular budget of the Health Department for the travel allowances and fuel expenses of the health minister.

◆

Chapter Eight

It Pays to be Sick

Going by the official records of parliament, Nepal appears to be ruled by sick politicians. A large number of parliament members have misused the special medical facilities provided to them by the government. In fact, they were seen playing the game of outpacing each other in pocketing money for purposes other than medical. Starting from Rs. 10,000, they were permitted allowances up to Rs. 300,000 for treatment of real or fictitious ailments.

A list of 60 (out of 265) members of the parliament was published along with the amount of money they had received from the government for treatment. The list has mentioned the speaker, chairmen of different committees, ministers, opposition leaders and ordinary members. It is an authentic list verified by no less a body than the Public Accounts Committee. The misused medical privileges looked so scandalous that the committee chose to banish the list to cold storage. But later under public pressure, it was made accessible.

The most interesting feature of this incredible phenomenon is that the parliamentarians have claimed to have taken the most expensive antibiotic. According to expert opinion, this medicine is administered only when the patient is so serious that he is confined to bed. But none of the members of the parliament had been so seriously ill in the last couple of years. The local press invariably carries the news of these VIPs getting admitted to the hospital even for a minor complaint. No such public information is available on 'very ill' lawmakers save a few. The fact that the prescriptions and the pharmaceutical bills of about forty MPs should contain the same expensive medicine cannot be a mere coincidence.

Many MPs were found, in this business of maximising benefits, forging their paperwork. One MP submitted a prescription issued by the Outdoor Patient Department testifying serious lung infection that would, if true, have forced him to bed for several weeks. In another case, a discrepancy was detected between the doctor's prescription and the bills submitted for reimbursement.

The papers submitted by yet another MP showed that he consulted a cardiologist purportedly for a lung disease and got his claims upheld. Some went ahead with only the purchase bills unaccompanied by prescriptions. Some members did even not bother to attach prescriptions to their claims for reimbursements.

The papers of one MP showed that he had a temperature of 162 degrees which is simply ridiculous because then he would be dead. He knew his carelessness would never be challenged by any official. One male MP got even paid for maternity care.

There is another variety of payment that has been made. One MP was paid for one bottle of Horlicks, one shampoo and one packet of tea. Another MP was paid for his room heater and cooler. Even the publicity materials of one MP were paid for as a medical item. The bills for fruit juice and liver too were included. One MP received payment for his medical treatment in Vellore, India, sitting at home. The number of MPs visiting the US and other countries for socalled medical check-ups gets inflated every year.

It is estimated that more than Rs. 10 million went to the medical treatment of the MPs who in fact were never sick. There are several agencies like the Cabinet Secretariat, the Home Ministry and the Parliament Secretariat which release the medical expenses to the lawmakers. There are, of course, rules that govern claims for medical expenses. The Medical Board that assesses the seriousness of the medical problem of an MP is invariably ignored or circumvented by the government.

The rules also decree that proper medical papers like the doctor's prescription, pathological test papers and medicine purchase bills are duly submitted along with the claim. But the rules are waived because the claimants are honourable men. On close scrutiny, it was discovered that in most cases the illnesses were faked and the papers fraudulent and the truth is that they took public money for personal benefit.

◆

Chapter Nine

Make Hay while the Sun Shines

The lawmakers of Nepal have treated themselves to special privileges and perks through odious legislation. Despite widespread public criticism of their self-seeking dispositions, the people's representatives try to justify the unjustifiable in the name of public duty. They not only display abrasiveness in getting legislation passed to serve their personal interests but also blatantly violate the spirit of the very regulations they make.

Some examples of such a gross misuse of power and privileges are:

1. One MP took thousands of rupees from the government treasury as reimbursement for the tips he gave bearers and taxi drivers during his trip to Bangkok. It is very unlikely that a Nepali will spend thousands of rupees in tipping. Although fake, the claim was entertained because he was an honourable member of parliament.

2. One lady MP produced a bill of Rs. 80,000 paid to a local traditional pharmacist for herbal medicine. With that amount, one can actually buy a whole shop of herbal medicines. It was a clear case of forgery but the bill was entertained as she too was honourable.

3. One MP made the government pay Rs. 45,000 for naturopathy at a local centre. To spend that kind of money for nature cure, which is by far the cheapest in Nepal, he would have to undergo treatment for decades.

4. One MP got Rs. 38,000 paid for herbal medicines by submitting fake bills. Herbal medicines are the cheapest

and the amount paid is glaring.

5. Another MP charged *Rs.* 18,000 for similar herbal medicines on the strength of similarly forged documents.

6. One MP got paid Rs. 18,000 for three injections (coramin) normally used for reviving the dying. He was never that seriously ill. It was a case of a fake claim entertained without question.

7. One MP got himself paid for four bottles of Horlicks, a nutritious drink which is not considered a medicine and moreover does not cost more than Rs. 1,000. But since he made a claim under the medical privilege, he was not denied reimbursement. That is demonstrative of how low the honourable members could stoop.

8. One MP was paid for fifty-six bottles of saline water. He must have been a hopeless medical case to need so many bottles of saline water. The said MP was never seriously sick. The claim was entertained as it was presented by the honourable member of parliament.

9. One MP got *Rs.* 50,000 paid having purchased medicines from a health post in a remote area. A health post never maintains such a large stock of medicines. In fact, a health post is allocated Rs. 20,000 to Rs. 30,000 for medicines for the whole year.

10. One male MP got paid for using medicines administered only to women during pre and post-delivery care.

11. Another MP got Rs. 46,000 paid for medicines purchased from a village pharmacy. It cannot but be a thoroughly fictitious deal.

12. One MP claimed Rs. 90,000 for a hospital room at the rate of Rs. 3,000 a day but for medicines he claimed only Rs. 1,500. It looks completely incongruous as there is no nursing home in Nepal where room charges are that high.

13. One MP claimed Rs. 10,000 as travel allowance for a day's travel to his village in between two official .meetings in Kathmandu. The amount is too little for helicopter service and too much for other means of transportation. It was no

doubt a spurious claim but nevertheless entertained.

14. One MP got Rs. 24,000 for a medical check-up by a doctor at the rate of Rs. 4,000 per visit. No doctor charges that much. The usual doctor's fee ranges from Rs. 100 to Rs. 200 in Nepal.

15. Another MP made a claim of Rs. 10,000 for telephone calls he made from outside Kathmandu to arrange for a vehicle to fetch him at the airport. An airport limousine costs only Rs. 300 for the Nepalese.

16. A group of MPs charged Rs. 90,000 for lunch they had during a meeting convened to deliberate on the civil service act. The truth is the meeting was not held for want of a quorum.

17. One MP charged Rs. 48,000 for mineral water. A bottle of mineral water costs only Rs. 15 in Nepal. Firstly, the mineral water is not covered by the 'privilege'. Secondly, it would take ages for him to consume mineral water worth all that money.

18. Another MP charged Rs. 75,000 for snacks. He was duly paid even though it was a bogus claim.

19. MPs have their personal assistants paid by the government. Instead of hiring qualified assistants they give the job to their own family members.

◆

Chapter Ten

The Secret Gifts

Although short of finances, the Nepalese government gives secret gifts to its poor and helpless citizens. If you are sick and have no money to pay for the medicines or hospital bills you can approach the Home Ministry for help. If you have gone broke while in the capital and have no money to travel back to your village you can approach the ministry for financial assistance.

This fund is very appropriately called the Fund for Economic Assistance, Donation, and Awards. The government sets aside an amount for this purpose. In 1997, the Fund had Rs. 7 million to its name. But the fund was gone before the year was out. So, fresh allotment was sought and an additional grant of Rs. 4 million was approved by the cabinet.

At first sight, it would appear that the government is generous to the poor and the helpless. Just the contrary is true.

A set of criteria has been devised to administer the fund but whatever is doled out is not subject to scrutiny by the state auditors. A maximum of Rs. 500 can be granted to a needy individual who then becomes ineligible for this assistance for three months. The donation is meant strictly for the disabled, the sick, and the poor who are required to prove themselves donation-worthy by a local body like the municipality or village council. The sick can receive a maximum of Rs. 1,000 on presentation of medical prescriptions. Similarly, social organisations can be given up to Rs. 50,000.

But records show that none of the criteria has been followed. Donations ranging from Rs. 5,000 to Rs. 800,000 have in fact been arbitrarily granted to different individuals. It was discovered that people no less than ministers themselves have bagged this secret gift presumably in the belief that the deal will never be made public. But it came to light when parliament's Public Accounts Committee investigated allegations to the effect that the fund was being misappropriated.

Records show that one home minister distributed Rs. four million within three months to his political henchmen and close associates. When the fund was draining, it was decided that not more than Rs. 50,000 would be granted in one day. When the fund started falling behind the rising demand, a more stringent regulation was followed. Accordingly, a maximum amount of Rs. 20,000 could be granted in one day. A further restraint was imposed disallowing more than Rs. 1,000 to one person seeking such contingency assistance.

At one time, the home minister delegated the power to his deputy. The deputy, in this case the Minister of State for Home, pocketed the major part of the fund by manipulating papers and faking signatures. He granted Rs. 1,000 to a person whose citizenship certificate was attached with his application. The rest of the money went to fictitious applicants. The money went straight to the State Minister's coffers. Since this fund is not properly accounted for like other official funds, it is not possible for anybody to have the thugs penalised in a court of law, and since the ministers themselves are involved, no one knows what can be done.

An authentic list of the names and amount of donations received from this fund was made public. According to the revelation, a home minister, himself a millionaire, bagged more than Rs. 300,000 and his deputy over Rs. 70,000. Other ministers' loot ranged from Rs. 150,000 to Rs. 50,000. The long list does not spare the honourable members of the parliament. The list of unidentified men and women from different parts of the country who have benefited from this secret gift is endless. Their 'takes' range from Rs. 100,000 to Rs. 300,000. Isn't this a glaring testimony to what extent public money is embezzled by those in power?

◆

Chapter Eleven

Reaping the Harvest

Political sufferers have a special connotation in the Nepalese society. Who are the sufferers and who made them suffer? Its antecedents go back to 1950s political changeover from one-family rule of the Ranas to a democratic system. The political activists who lost their lives or properties were later compensated by the state with 4 bighas (2.8 hectares) of land each in the Terai. It was a kind of political recognition of their role in bringing democracy to Nepal. Since many of them were well past their working age and not able to earn any more, the land donation as an old-age pension was greeted by the people with appreciation.

The second wave of political sufferers emerged during 1960-1990 when the King ruled the country with absolute power. The political opponents of this system belonged mainly to the Congress or Communist groups who operated underground for thirty years. Some of them died in jail, some were shot dead without trial, some went into exile to India. The state instituted cases of treason and sedition against these political activists and seized their properties.

However, the administration, while designing the auction rules governing the confiscated properties, made sure that the properties went to the close relatives of the political victims. The price was fixed in such a way that it was within the financial reach of the families concerned. At a time when the market price of one bigha (about 0.6 hectares) of land was around Rs. 10,000, a 20-bigha (13.5 hectares) plot of land, confiscated from a political rebel, was offered to his near relative for Rs. 1,000 at the rate of Rs. 100 per bigha. Since there was no political freedom and no freedom of speech and press, nobody dared question the arbitrary decision of the government.

After the 1990 changeover, the practice of compensating political sufferers resumed. This time it was not land which was offered in compensation. It was cash. The claims were of course highly exaggerated. One political victim claimed that he had lost 15 quintals of silver and 600 tolas (6,648 gr) of gold. The claim though unbelievable in the context of the general Nepalese standard of living was partially accepted. A lump sum of Rs. 1.2 million was paid to the 'victim'.

In a similar case, a political sufferer claimed to have lost 20,000 silver coins. In the olden days, the government issued one-rupee silver coins. As the market price of silver shot up and the face value of the coin went down, the people preserved the coins to fetch a better price at a later date. Again, there was no evidence that the erstwhile administration had really confiscated 20,000 silver coins of his. The post-1990 government paid him for the 'lost' coins at the going market rate.

In this way, the government paid Rs. 25 million in one year to the political sufferers. The compensation process was handled by a prominent leader of the prominent political party rather than by an official agency. The government paid nearly Rs. 100 million to him to use it at his discretion. How it was administered is known only to him. Neither the government nor the public has any knowledge of how it was finally used. No question was asked about it. The government still continues regularly to grant political compensation through him. Perhaps rightly, the Nepalese believe that a political career after all is not a bad investment. Every dog has his day. On your day, millions of rupees are at your personal disposal.

◆

Chapter Twelve

The Golden Airport

Let us think of about four thousand kilograms of gold passing clandestinely through Nepal's only international airport in Kathmandu every month. For this shady deal, let us imagine that the importers pay Rs. 80 to Rs. 180 million to powerful ministers every month. Because it is kept out of the official records, the government gets no revenue at all out of this mind-boggling cargo. It sounds rather incredible but that is what everybody was talking about in Nepal in the beginning of 1998. The public believe the story to be true. One estimate puts the import of gold to be worth Rs. 50 billion, of which half was legally brought in and the other half illegally let in within a period of just four months at the end of 1997. The practice continues unabated with no serious steps taken to stop it.

When gold smuggling was raised in parliament, the government did not deny it. On the contrary, the prime minister, the finance minister and the home minister who were accused of colluding in this nefarious act tacitly admitted its incidence but passed the buck on to nebulous unidentifiable political elements. Mutual mud-slinging ensued among the powerful ministers who held important portfolios. They were all just short of naming the names which were more or less known already. After an uproar in parliament, a committee of investigation was constituted but the people thought it an eyewash. The real culprits were not captured because the government itself was widely perceived to be party to the illegal act.

The gold trade is very lucrative in Nepal. It is always dealt in cash as the Nepalese economy is basically a cash economy.

However, tonnes of gold come to Nepal which are not actually meant for the Nepalese market which does not have the capacity to absorb the huge quantity of gold that is illegally imported. It is actually meant for the Indian market where it fetches a higher price. That explains why the business thrives.

Smuggling on such a large scale is considered unthinkable without official patronage and connivance. Stories published in the newspapers give a blow by blow account of smuggling in the country. According to one account, when the aircraft lands at the Tribhuwan International Airport the passengers disembark and proceed to immigration and customs counters. A bunch of official loaders enter the luggage cabin to unload the baggage. While unloading they see that the gold-laden suitcases are unloaded last and the contraband is transferred to an official vehicle on the waiting tarmac. When the luggage trolley pulls up towards the customs bay it stops midway to have the 'golden' consignments transferred to the waiting vehicle without any hassle. The vehicle makes a turn and exits from the airport unchecked.

It is difficult not to believe because the news report publishes the flight number, the names of the loaders and the number of vehicles sneaking out with gold trunks. A report recounts that passengers carrying gold bars in person and well known to the customs officers have been whisked away in an official vehicle through a special gate. The goods are delivered to a loader's home. The vehicle, the loader and the location of his home are all included in the story.

In yet another instance, Qatar Airways - which operates three flights a week to Kathmandu - brings 300 to 500 kg of gold in every flight. The passengers leave the plane by buses. The buses come back to take the gold containers to an exclusive area where an official vehicle awaits. The vehicle leaves the airport with armed official guards. In this case also everyone involved, including the police and customs officers, has been identified and the vehicle number mentioned.

There are 'innumerable other episodes reported in the local press mainly describing how gold smugglers make an exit from the airport without passing through immigration and customs checkpoints. They are said to be escorted by security and customs officials and let out through special gates meant for authorised airport personnel only.

In one instance, a passenger carrying 10 kg of gold tried to pass through the green channel. The custom officials ignored the metal beeps on the screen but the police officials stopped him for a body search. The passenger was, however, let free after paying Rs. 300,000 as import duty. According to the regulations, his gold had to be confiscated. Had that been done, the government would have made Rs. 6.4 million. It turned out that the smuggler was a regular carrier in league with the custom officials at the airport.

In another instance, the Pakistani authorities in Karachi tipped the Nepalese customs about a gold carrier on board a PIA flight from Dubai to Kathmandu via Karachi. When the man was nabbed at the exit point he had nothing on his person. He confessed however that the 10 kg of gold he was carrying was taken by somebody at the transit lounge as planned. The whole episode was not as mysterious as it was made out to be.

The smuggling of gold and other merchandise through this golden airport of Nepal is so frequent and well known that currently there are representatives of as many as thirteen government agencies to supervise it. According to popular belief, all of them have become the shareholders in the smuggling booty. It would not have been possible without political patronage and involvement of powerful figures in the government.

◆

Chapter Thirteen

Vehicles for Vegetables

The four wheeler has always been a sensitive issue in Nepal. Vehicle possession is a facility not common to all. In the government, it is only the high officials who are entitled to this facility. Privately, it is only a few of the rich industrialists, businessmen, doctors and professionals who can afford to own a car. Thus a vehicle is a symbol of affluence, power or privilege. For the Nepalese, it is not just a transport facility. It carries a lot more meaning in terms of their status, sentimentality and sensitivity. The government treats it as a luxury item. With this in mind, the government has been levying high tariffs on its import, at one time as much as 300% of the factory price.

Way back in 1973, the vehicle issue flared up in a big way. The matter came to a head when government vehicles were seen at vegetable markets, temples and entertainment spots, and transporting kids to and fro. The government had provided the facility to the officials to carry out their official duties and responsibilities efficiently. A resource-constrained government could not foot the bill for a vehicle used purely for personal and recreational purposes. At that point the government was bearing Rs. 4 million to meet the cost of fuel for official vehicles.

King Birendra, at the start of his rule, wanted to curb the misuse. With that objective in mind, a committee was formed to regulate vehicular use. The committee came up with a set of recommendations that imposed restrictions on the use of official vehicles. The officials resisted the reforms but finally had to give in when the King appeared adamant about it. Some of the secretaries started walking to and from their office as a mark of protest against the curbs. Government vehicles were nabbed by the police on weekends and public holidays as part of the programme to combat misuse. It worked for some time but misuse resumed under a different set of pretexts.

With the decline in the absolute power and authority of the King, the misuse of government vehicles got out of hand. Many officials used official vehicles, the drivers and fuel for personal benefit. The politicians, especially the ministers, started having a fleet of cars, jeeps and station wagons pulled out of big development projects. The Nepal Electricity Authority, for example, which had about two hundred vehicles in its inventory had given away fifty of them to the ministers and members of parliament. There is hardly any project which has not surrendered its vehicles to the demand of local executives and leaders, the ministers and members of parliament.

The political change from absolute monarchy to parliamentary democracy in 1990 made it all the worse. It was around 1995 that the misuse of the privilege peaked. All members of the parliament, high government officials, royal palace functionaries and members of the constitutional bodies were granted in one fell swoop the facility to import one vehicle per head duty free. When most of the privileged people brought in the Japan-made Pajero, the Nepalese people were quick to dub the parliamentary democracy a *pajero* democracy. This facility cost the government about $20 million in net revenue losses. As a mark of public resentment against this highly questionable decision some angry citizens vandalised some Pajeros parked in open street. But the resentment faded away and the Pajero prevailed.

Public resentment has however not subsided. In a few incidents extreme left elements have attacked these sleek vehicles causing severe damage. There is a lurking fear among the owners of this luxurious endowment that the public ire may some day explode into violent incidents. The fear is however not unfounded as the political extremists have warned that they would not only express their disgust against misuse of power but also penalise the guilty by taking the law in their own hands. The Pajero has symbolically triggered a wave of widespread discontent against those in the privileged bracket. But it may have a snowballing effect on the basic tenets of parliamentary democracy which appears fragile under the weight of consistent misuse of power and authority.

◆

Chapter Fourteen

A Salivating Waiver

In 1996, when the government under the premiership of Sher Bahadur Deuba was constantly hounded by the legislators in the hung parliament, he conceded an unprecedented privilege to them. He allowed the import of vehicles of their choice free of customs and sales taxes. The move was no doubt motivated by the need to silence his detractors in parliament. A vehicle normally costing a million rupees in the market could be had at one third of the price. Since Nepal has no automobile manufacturing or assembly plant every vehicle and its necessary parts has to be imported. When you import you can choose the best out of several options. With the concessions granted by the government, Nepal witnessed a sudden rush of sleek Japanese and British motor vehicles on the roads.

This state facility was granted to members of both the houses of parliament, Supreme Court judges, heads and members of constitutional bodies, high army and police officials, top officials at the royal palace and secretaries, and other special-class officials in the government. Altogether the number of such 'high' officials at that time was around 600. However, there were some who refused to take advantage of the facility out of individual conscience or morality. All of these important persons draw salary, allowance and perks from the national treasury according to their status and seniority. The parliamentarians have legislated themselves to pension eligibility for life like any permanent civil servant. The vehicle import facility was an extra incentive, as if they did not already have enough.

The Pajero, a product of the Mitsubishi Company of Japan, or the Prado, a Toyota Landcruiser, became the favourite choice of most of the overnight rich representatives of the poor people of Nepal. The highest priced vehicle was worth Rs. 3.4 million fitted with the latest computerised comforts and the lowest one was priced at Rs. 600,000. The average cost of the vehicles was around Rs. 2 million. So, in every vehicle imported the government lost revenue amounting to Rs. 2 million. The government lost Rs. 1,200 million in the import of the 600 vehicles under this tantalising scheme. At the current rate the loss to national exchequer was a cool $20 million.

Questions with respect to sources of money were raised. Where and how did people in high places get the money to pay for such expensive vehicles? Since the government itself was encouraging unfair practices, there was no one who would push this issue to its logical conclusion. The unspoken rule was 'amass wealth by whatever means', fair or unfair. Those who could not normally afford it became abnormally resourceful once the concession was announced. Legitimising the illegitimate wealth became the main occupation, and it was done with no qualms of conscience.

The story however did not end there. It is the widespread misuse rather than the use of these 'subsidised' vehicles that has raised eyebrows. Various types of misuse came to light. First, the vehicles were actually sold to businessmen at a premium price letting both the buyers and sellers make a profit out of the deal. In fact, the benefit margin of Rs. 2 million (in other words, the direct loss to the national treasury) of each vehicle was shared by both parties. It was discovered in practice that more than half of these vehicles were being driven by somebody other than the actual importers.

Second, most of the people's representatives and officials have government vehicles. The rule says that those who have been given the import facility would not be allowed to use official vehicles. But the rule is far from enforced. Most of them who have taken advantage of the import privilege continue to use official vehicles. People enjoying this facility twice is not an unfamiliar phenomenon.

Third, some powerful people, as they continue to use the official vehicle, have meanwhile rented out their duty-free vehicles to government projects at a fairly high price. It was reported that the rental for such a vehicle fetches as much as Rs. 60,000 per month. The development projects were coerced by the powerful ones to take their vehicles on rent. It is single, double and, in some cases, even triple benefits to those in the legislature, the judiciary and the bureaucracy. The nation is the loser.

◆

Chapter Fifteen

Allowance Par Excellence

Misuse of funds by Foreign Ministry officials abroad is not unheard of in Nepal. The biggest scandal took place in Japan a couple of decades ago when a huge donation offered by the Japanese for the development of Lumbini, the birth place of Lord Buddha, was misappropriated by the then resident Nepalese ambassador.

The Tibet loot was all the more legendary. When the Chinese took over Tibet and the Dalai Lama fled his country in 1958, the resident Nepalese businessmen too had to flee. Those who had amassed wealth in Tibet dumped all their valuables in the Nepalese mission under assurance that they would get the valuables back in Kathmandu. The Chinese authorities in Tibet indeed allowed the Nepalese officials to transfer truckloads of goods under diplomatic cover. But none of the valuables was ever returned to their legitimate owners, nor did they go to the government treasury. The unscrupulous officials became rich overnight. The consignment was composed mainly of gold ornaments, antiques and precious stones.

Compared to this epochal haul of property loot, irregular practices and misuse of funds elsewhere look like peanuts. But it reveals the common nature of misuse of funds at this level. Listed below are some of the authenticated cases.

1. Nepal sent a big twenty-three-member delegation to the United Nations General Assembly in 1997, whereas in the preceding years the number did not usually exceed five. Since there was no way the government could Justify this, it did not have the moral courage even to make a public

announcement of who was in the delegation which it normally did.

The daily allowance paid to the 'delegates' alone came to about $130,000. If the government had stuck to the usual number of five, $30,000 would have sufficed. On top of it, the airfare bill for twenty-three cost the country another $46,000. For five members it would have been a tolerable $10,000. So the government ended up squandering $136,000 extra in this unnecessary venture.

2. The government pays full fare, instead of a discounted one, for international passage for one good reason. The officials get 9% commission from the travel agents. So on the surface, no irregularity is observed as the government pays the standard fare. On private visits, nobody pays full fare.

3. An ambassador to Moscow took a personal assistant at the state's expense but upon arrival he hired the same person as a local employee for seven months and paid him $3,500. A local employee does not travel at the expenses of the country the ambassador comes from. If he went as an assistant to the envoy, he cannot be employed as a local.

4. The government pays for the travel of the ambassador's spouse and two children below the age of twenty-one. But the new constitution of Nepal has reduced the adulthood age from twenty-one to eighteen. Irrespective of this change in basic law, the government continues to pay the dependence allowance to the children up to the age of twenty-one.

5. The spouse gets the foreign allowance at the rate of ten per cent of the employee's salary. The first child gets the same amount but the second child gets half of that. There is nothing wrong in this regulation. The problem is they keep receiving the allowance even if they stay in the home country. Similarly, the father or mother of the diplomat is allowed the same kind of facility. But there are many instances when he or she is back home, drawing the foreign allowance unhindered.

There have been cases where the family members take the air tickets from the government but instead of travelling to the foreign destination, they return the same to the travel agents for personal reimbursements.

6. The accounts of the Ministry of Foreign Affairs have not been audited for the last ten years. That speaks for the extent of mismanagement of national resources.

7. The government raises a considerable amount of money from visa fees paid by visitors to Nepal. Misuse is suspected as there is no system to verify if all of it goes to the national treasury.

8. The Nepalese embassies in Bonn and London in 1996 misused Rs. 1 million, which was returned to them by the German government on account of Value Added Tax. The VAT as such should be deposited in the Nepalese treasury instead of going into individual's pockets.

9. The Ministry of Foreign Affairs in 1996 overpaid Rs. 136,000 in a procurement deal of Rs. 518,000.

10. The Ministry of Foreign Affairs received fifteen cars from South Korea as a gift without the knowledge of the Finance Ministry. Some of these cars which started with white government plates were later converted into private vehicles.

11. One retired chief of protocol has not cleared Rs. 15 million he had taken as an advance from the Foreign Ministry. Similarly, a former ambassador and a military attache have also not settled the accounts of Rs. 1 million against their names, even after leaving office.

12. The Nepalese missions abroad have spent Rs. 15 million in international calls. It is believed that most calls were of a personal nature.

13. An ambassador to Myangmar took daily allowances and travel expenses without moving out. Similarly, the family members of an official in the same mission took travel allowances not authorised by law.

◆

Chapter Sixteen

The Other Way Round

According to the Nepalese laws, all land belongs to the state. The right to private land property is not inviolable in the sense that the government can acquire the private land for public use by paying compensation. But in practice, it is the other way round. It is the individuals who acquire public land by illegal means, and get it sanctioned by law over a period of time.

When Nepal was rich in forest resources in the 1960s and 1970s, the King doled out plot after plot of forest and public land to his courtiers and favourite officials as a matter of personal favour. The royal donation of an abandoned airport in Biratnagar to a high government official is a classic example of the extent to which the 'royal pleasure' can go.

In a typical case of illegal land grab, the anti-corruption agency of the government found that Rishi Kumar Pandey, a high official, had grabbed about 1,112 ropanies (56 hectares) in the Chaturale village in the Nuwakot district. The investigation discovered that the land, almost half a mountain of forested area, was registered in his and his family members' names.

According to the law, no forested land, irrespective of its being fenced or not, or land surrounded by forest can be registered in an individual's name. The land in question was officially recorded as forest land. Pandey was found guilty of getting it registered in his and his family's name in connivance with the officials of the Land Revenue Office.

The land grab was illegal from yet another angle. The law says no individual is allowed to hold more than eighty ropanies of land in the hills. (One hectare is equal to 19.66 ropanies and one ropani is equal to 0.05 hectares.) Land beyond that is automatically seized by the government for redistribution to the landless peasants. An individual can hold land above the limit for the purpose of building an industry or some other approved reason.

In this case, no such permission had been obtained. Moreover, the Land Revenue Office was found guilty of not referring the matter to the Land Reforms Office, a separate department of the government.

Pandey was aware of this land-limit provision. To circumvent the regulation, he transferred the ownership of the property to an orchard company belonging to himself. However, the investigation found the ownership transfer irregular because it was effected only after the orchard company came into existence.

With all this evidence, the anti-corruption agency filed the case with the Department of Forests and the Department of Land Revenue, asking them to revoke the registration and penalise the erring officials who had converted state property into a private one. But no action was ever taken by the government.

In yet another case, the anti-corruption agency unearthed the embezzlement of public funds disbursed to pay compensation to the villagers. It was in Rolpa, a remote district in west Nepal where the literacy is extremely low. The villagers are very afraid of government officials, the police and the army, who symbolise terror and downright exploitation.

In that district, the government decided to build an army barrack on private land. The government has to follow a process in acquiring private land for public use. The Chief District Officer (CDO) is primarily responsible for completing the process.

The private land belonged to seven villagers. An evaluation committee was formed by the CDO to determine the rate of compensation to the villagers concerned. The price was officially fixed at Rs. 1.7 million. But the CDO actually paid only Rs. 1 million to the villagers. The remaining Rs. 700,000 was pocketed by him and his collaborators.

On investigation by the anti-corruption agency it was revealed that the whole payment was made in cash and not through cheques which is the standard procedure when public money is involved. It is established that Rs. 1.7 million was cashed by the CDO who called the villagers to his home after office hours, paid them Rs. 1 million but made them sign for Rs. 1.7 million.

Later the villagers admitted in their statements that they either could not properly read the documents or dared not question the discrepancy for fear they might be victimised under this or that pretext. It was also disclosed that one official told the villagers that if they kept mum they would eventually be compensated with free land somewhere in the same village.

The anti-corruption agency framed a case of embezzlement of public money against three officials including the CDO. The judicial court's verdict in the case is still awaited.

◆

Chapter Seventeen

Petty but Poignant

The government has made suitable provisions for its employees on out-station duty. Besides daily allowances, they are provided special allowances to compensate for the distance they have to cover on foot as modern means of transport are not available in most of the mountainous parts of Nepal.

In an interesting case revealed in 1995 by the Auditor General's Office, two overseers of the District Irrigation Office of Nuwakot were found guilty of indulging in something extraordinary. They were entitled one cook and one porter each during the period of their inspection tour of the area assigned to them. They hired five cooks and twenty porters each.

By no stretch of imagination could they justify it. It is simply unthinkable in the Nepalese context for an overseer to have the luxury of five cooks, nor he can have so much luggage and equipment requiring twenty porters. Personal effects including the bed and blankets can easily be carried by one or at most two porters.

It was obvious that the roster of cooks and porters was fake and the allowance drawn against their names went into the overseers' pockets. The net loss to the treasury on this account was Rs. 17,000 ($400). The amount may appear small but the situation certainly is outrageous.

The overseers have been officially asked to return the money purportedly paid to the cooks and porters.

There is yet another interesting case involving some thirty policemen. The world knows that a serious problem of girl trafficking exists in Nepal. As many as two hundred thousand young girls are believed to be working in brothels of some Indian cities. Rasuwa, a neighbouring district of Kathmandu, is one of the districts from where these girls are 'exported' to India and elsewhere.

The police have the main responsibility of monitoring and controlling girl trafficking at the border, as well as in the supplying districts. In the face of virulent public reaction, the police force has been forced to launch a special programme to control the crime. It was in this connection that a group of thirty policemen toured the villages of Rasuwa for three days.

The rules say that their travel allowances would be determined on the basis of the distance they cover. The police contingent said it covered twenty-eight miles on the first day, thirty-two miles on the second day and thirty-six miles on the third day. They were paid accordingly.

But the Auditor General objected to the fact that it was impossible for anybody, in including the robust policemen, to cover such a long distance in three days. If true, they must have jogged non-stop over the mountains of which the district is made up.

Even if one were to grant that the policemen did indeed travel the distance they claimed, they failed to address the problem they had been assigned to tackle. Girl trafficking cannot be controlled just by walking on village roads, which the policemen had apparently done.

The Auditor General has taken a strong exception to the misuse of government funds to the tune of Rs. 33,000.

However he did not ask the policemen to return the money, despite the failure on their part to answer the charge.

These are only examples. The 500-page report of the Auditor General is full of such ingenious ways of squeezing the state treasury for personal gain. The cases cited may look small in amount but are very poignant when judged in terms of public morality. By no means are the examples few and far between. Their recurrence, year in and year out, is phenomenal.

◆

Chapter Eighteen

The Leaking Vessels

Nepal has been a witness to a strange phenomenon of thriving business houses collapsing overnight and commercial companies vanishing from the scene. Successful enterprises, instead of boosting their business and credibility, suddenly go out of existence. Why?

The reason is not so far to seek. The sudden collapse or disappearance is actually staged to evade taxes. The Auditor General's report of 1997, taking note of this, has asked the government to collect taxes from the defaulters within a time frame. But this has obviously fallen on deaf ears.

According to the Auditor General's Office, a large amount to the tune of Rs. 3,460 million ($57 million) remained to be collected in 1996.

The Auditor General felt that there were enough legal provisions to make the defaulters pay the taxes. The government can take severe actions like seizing defaulters' property, closing business, auctioning assets, and throwing them behind bars. But no such action appears to have been initiated against the tax evaders.

Political instability is often blamed for weak financial administration. In 1998, there was a visible slump in revenue collection, by one third. The lost revenue was estimated to be Rs. 7 billion. The revenue collection from Nepal's only international airport went down by 30%, a clear loss of Rs. 500 million. It was attributed to open racketeering at the airport with the express approval of some powerful ministers. Not that the volume of international trade had gone down. The fact is that the legal trade was diverted through illegal channels. That way the government may have lost the revenue but government officials and political leaders profited from it.

On the contiguous southern border with India, the illegal trade and transactions are planned and supervised by Mafia groups. Many a group of operators assured a safe delivery of goods to Nepal by bypassing all customs formalities. These groups charged a service fee which is much less than one would end up paying the government. For example, they would charge Rs. 1 million for the consignments which would otherwise cost a businessman Rs. 5 million in customs duty. The operation has been made possible by corrupt politicians and officials hand in glove with the traders. The net result is a sharp decline in national income.

The revenue leakage is a perennial source of concern for the Auditor General's Office. It reported a leakage in government revenue to the tune of Rs. 153 million in 1997. It was, in its own words, just the tip of an iceberg. As the auditing of government accounts is carried out on a sampling basis rather than on detailed documentation due to manpower constraints, the detection of leakage is only an indication of what actually transpires in the financial regime.

In a country where the contribution of national resources to annual state expenditure is less than sixty per cent, it is all the more galling to see the revenue being cut by unscrupulous means. In many cases, the actual customs and sales tax collection is far less than the regulations demand. It is partly because the goods are arbitrarily placed in a less revenue-paying category. No attention is paid to cost evaluation of the industrial goods resulting in reduced level of revenue generation.

Fines are often waived, again on questionable grounds. These weaknesses are actually not human weaknesses. They are popular devices to deprive the government of legitimate revenue and enrich the corrupt officials. Small wonder then that there is tough competition among the government officials to get assigned to the revenue-oriented departments like the Income Tax office, the Customs Office and the Excise and Sales Tax Office.

It is the political intervention designed to raise money from plum sources that has played havoc with the fiscal health of Nepal. The fear that the country may indeed go bankrupt in the near future is not entirely misplaced.   ◆

Chapter Nineteen

A National Pet

Sociologically Nepal is a mixed bag of distinct and independent communities. Despite the political integration and unified civil codes, these communities exercise a great deal of autonomy and independence. The grass-roots social organisations are the natural outcome of this phenomenon. They are self-reliant, self-regulated and self-sustaining. Over the centuries they did not meddle with politics of power and were therefore left alone. However, when the democratic process started to grip the Nepalese society and the foreign money began to flow in, a new set of independent organisations called NGOs (non-governmental organisations) sprouted all over Nepal.

The assumption is that apart from the governmental organisations, there always are non-governmental organisations functioning in juxtaposition with each other, that were technically accepted by the Nepalese. But they were brought under strict and stringent political control during the 1960-1990 period because *ipso facto* they represented individual and organisational freedom which though incorporated in the constitution was denied in practice. When political freedom was achieved in 1991, the floodgate of NGOs opened and they all came rushing down.

An NGO is a pet for all, high or low, in or out of the government. It starts from the King of Nepal, who controls an NGO as its patron. He nominates its chairman who in turn nominates the members of the governing board. Since there is no system of elections nor a system of enlisting members in this particular organisation, it is perpetually a King-controlled outfit in the non-governmental sector.

The Queen is not far behind. She also heads an NGO that looks after the development of the most holy shrine of Nepal, Pashupatinath Temple. Until she quits of her own volition, she cannot be asked to vacate the seat. Many members of the royal family of Nepal were heading some leading NGOs before the changeover in 1990. They preferred to leave the limelight only after the King's powers were clipped.

Even the government owns an NGO. The Social Welfare Council, a national co-ordination body of the Nepalese NGOs, is headed by none other than a Minister. Hundreds of NGOs are affiliated to this body for varying purposes.

Many government officials are also closely involved in NGOs' activities. They directly or indirectly patronise these NGOs. The international funding agencies operating in Nepal also have their favourite organisations which have in fact been created at their behest.

There are, then, NGOs belonging to a family with its members in charge of resource management. There are of course those which just belong to some individuals. No wonder that Nepal is overcrowded with NGOs of all denominations.

There are more than 5,000 NGOs registered with the government. According to the regulations, every NGO has to renew the licence and to do so it has to submit annual programmes, accomplished activities, audited accounts and personal briefs of the portfolio holders. It is just a formality which is promptly forgotten. The government branch which deals with it has no manpower capability to monitor activities with seriousness.

Nobody, therefore, has a comprehensive idea of what the NGOs of Nepal are doing for the public good. Those who have made their presence felt with good performances are in the minority. Those that prefer to work unnoticed dealing with unknown areas of interest are, of course, in the majority.

How much funding has come from the foreign agencies nobody can tell. What kind of services have been delivered to the needy and how the job has been accomplished, there is no credible record of.

Primarily, the poor have been the target beneficiaries. But as things stand today, no doubt the 'poverty' of NGO managers has been taken care of but no one can say the same about the 'poverty' of the poor in Nepal. The wave of independent organisations nonetheless continues to overwhelm the country, the objective being to help the poor help themselves.

◆

Chapter Twenty

Price Tag

In Nepal everything is on sale. That is what one could gather from the pages of newspapers, hush-hush parleys in town and the sudden spurt in the vulgar exhibition of ill-gotten affluence. In a free market, of course, the prices fluctuate as demand and supply interact with each other. One can visualise Nepal as a big shopping complex where you can go on browsing through merchandise with the price tag dangling.

The most precious of all are, of course, the political players who can ask for any price. Their price touches incredible millions. The biggest price is quoted by the powerful parliamentarians who hold the key to the life or death of the incumbent administration. Because of the hung character of parliament after the 1993 national poll, no political party had the numbers to form a stable government.

The seven political parties represented in parliament went around revelling in the dictum that politics is a game of possibilities, including the possibility of minting money. The parliament was summoned to frequent special sessions to debate the vote of no-confidence and then the vote of confidence which inevitably led to intense horse-trading. More often than not an independent or a small party of two or three members in parliament decided the fate of the government. And they were the lead beneficiaries.

That is the time when the smallest in terms of number became the strongest. Naturally, they fetched the highest price for their support of whoever formed the government. Reports said they got paid between Rs. 5 million to Rs. 20 million, all from the national treasury. There are no credible grounds to disbelieve it. A former prime minister publicly admitted taking Rs 5 million for buying MPs. A cabinet berth itself as a reward was of little or no consequence to them as the government's longevity was far from assured. A down payment was infinitely better. The money could be used to consolidate the party they belonged to, or they could live a happy life ever after.

Those who stayed in power by paying such a high price made sure they too were adequately rewarded. Gold smuggling carried out with the tacit consent of the ministers in 1998 is a case in point. The beneficiaries were unofficially identified, but the allegations were never officially denied.

The prime minister was getting Rs. 40 million per month. About the same amount went to the leader of the party that was a main partner in the then coalition government. Among the shareholders were the home minister and the finance minister who gobbled Rs. 10 million each a month. Two top customs officials were getting Rs. 2.5 million each and their subordinates Rs. 1 million each, while the police officials facilitating the smuggling were given Rs. 500,000 each per month.

This was indeed a mind-boggling windfall that was not regarded as a sustainable source of bumper income for the ministers, as the subsequent hue and cry in parliament and public quarters led to legislative probes, to at least pacify the growing public resentment over the issue.

There is however a regular and firm source of hefty income from when ambassadors and general managers, directors and other officials of public corporations are appointed. People handling mega projects have no limit to their secret gains. But all of them, with perhaps a few exceptions, are well known for fixing price tags in lucrative public offices. A look at a sample of some openly discussed official appointments indeed makes interesting reading.

An ambassador was believed to have landed the plum job on payment of a few million rupees. The director generalship of customs, tax, and other revenue-oriented departments is considered a prize post. The price tags go above Rs. 5 million apiece. The director general of the Department of Irrigation is reportedly up for a bidder of Rs. 4 million. The same is the cost for the general managerships of big organisations associated with industrial loans, oil, trade, supplies etc.

At the lower echelons, the price tag naturally slides down. For example, a non-gazetted post at the airport is available at Rs. 300,000. Even an aspiring police recruit has to pay Rs. 10,000 to Rs. 15,000. For jobs in places like the international airport, the price is naturally a lot higher. The forest sector, well known for corruption, is pretty expensive. The post of district forest officer brings home over one million rupees to the person with the power to appoint.

The development projects are by far the most attractive of all. The project chief has to share the loot with his superiors. The higher the project cost the greater the benefits to the officials. That of course explains why the scramble for posts is so intense and why the frequency of transfer of personnel is so high.

At the grass-roots level, though the price might look too small, the benefit is taken for granted. Nepal being an agricultural country has numerous land-related officers whom the poor farmers have to deal with. Small bribes are thus an accepted norm. They do not raise any eyebrows in society. In many places bribes are prescribed. For example, a land registration paper costs Rs. 5; a land map an extra Rs. 20; and an adjustment made in the land record warrants Rs. 500. A land plot reallocation would need an extra payment of Rs. 200 to Rs. 1,000, whereas a land ownership certificate for the unrecorded plots would cost Rs. 10,000.

◆

the Swiss
implement
Darchula.
siderable
aterials

fully
too
xt?

r

.otting and Rusting

Darchula is one of Nepal's remote districts. Geographically rugged but politically sensitive, it borders the two belligerents of Asia- India and China. Kalapani, a part of Darchula district, has become a hotbed of controversy between Nepal and India. The Indian troops have been in occupation of this strategic area for decades. Nepal wants it vacated. The Chinese are next door; thankfully they have not poked their noses into this territorial matter.

People in Darchula still live a primitive life. Kathmandu is too far away to turn its attention and is not so keen on developing it. Until 1975 there was only one suspension bridge worth the name although numerous rivers crisscross the district. Development merchants in Kathmandu don't even seem aware of the district's immediate and desperate needs. The economic planners of Nepal, however, do allocate scant resources for this remote district to justify its existence.

In 1975, some funds were allocated for a suspension bridge over the Chaulane river in Darchula. The roads and bridge officials despatched an overseer to make a survey and recommend an appropriate site for the bridge. The overseer proposed a site for the 80m plus span. However, the fund wasn't there. The report was conveniently shelved to collect dust.

A few years later, funds became available under a Swiss assistance programme for the bridge. A Swiss engineer- cum-adviser was assigned to carry out the construction. Instead of sending a fresh team of surveyors to select the site, the authorities decided to resurrect the old report.

As all necessary data was there in the repo
gentleman and his Nepalese counterparts decided t
the report. A prefabricated bridge was transported to
Since there is no proper access road to the bridge site cor
difficulties were faced in getting cables and other i
transported over the mountains. Nevertheless, it was done.

But when the engineers and other technicians arrivec
equipped with bridge materials, they found that the span wa
short to cover the width of the river. They were in a fix. What n
They referred the matter over to the central authorities i
guidance. The technical team was told to lay the bridge wherever .
fitted. A site was finally found. Problem: there was no trail, no road
and no movement of people. But the bridge got there, to be used by
no one.

This matter was seriously objected to by the Auditor General
of Nepal. He made a big issue out of it and wanted the persons
responsible for putting the bridge down penalised under the law.
The Public Accounts Committee followed it up, but the overseer
and the technicians were saved by some members of the committee
with whom they had links, legitimate or otherwise. The blame was
laid on the survey equipment. The bridge stands there as a symbol
of folly, rotting and rusting as time goes by.

◆

PART III
Institutions, Mismanagement and Losses

Chapter Twenty-Two

Predators Within and Without

Can you believe that a big organisation like the Nepal Electricity Authority (NEA), in charge of almost all production and distribution of electricity in Nepal and having an annual turnover of billions of rupees, can operate without a single means of transport at its headquarters? It certainly cannot. Then, why is Nepal Electricity Authority (NEA) disposing of all vehicles in its possession? It is indeed a tricky measure initiated to address a tricky problem.

The problem is that being completely owned by the government, it has to abide by the orders of the water resources ministers (past, present and potential), high officials, and powerful members of the parliament. On orders from 'above' the vehicles that the NEA procures for its operations have to be supplied to whoever needs them for private use. It was discovered in the beginning of 1998 that in eight years since the dawn of parliamentary democracy in Nepal, some twenty-eight vehicles had vanished from its inventory.

The problem does not end there. The NEA has to pay for fuel and maintenance to the new users of its vehicles. About Rs. 30 million is squandered annually in this manner. When the vehicles that it owns but does not use meet with an accident, the NEA ends up footing the repair bill. Replacing the missing parts and replenishing the stolen or damaged spare parts is a regular phenomenon. So going by simple logic, the question arises: why should NEA buy vehicles which it does not use?

But of course, NEA cannot do without. It has to run its vehicles for normal operations in the field as well as at headquarters. As a way out it ruled that all the field vehicle be big and grotesque, not good enough to attract the powers that be. At headquarters, all the vehicles will either be privatised by its officials or sold out. There will be no yellow-plate vehicle at the centre (yellow denoting government corporation, red denoting private and white denoting government vehicles).

It is in this context that the NEA launched a scheme for its high-level employees to own a car. Accordingly, they are allowed to own the cars they have been using on official duty by paying the original price with ten per cent annual depreciation. That way, the NEA thought, nobody in the government or parliament would be able to ask for a 'privately owned' car from the organisation since they are only capable of misusing public property.

In order to rule out the possibility of the corporate vehicles being misused or lost, the NEA followed the policy of handing over vehicle ownerships to the user officials themselves. In case they want a new vehicle under the same conditions, they were allocated a lump sum of Rs. 120 million ($2 million) to buy about seventy-five new vehicles, each costing not more than Rs. 1.5 million. These officials, incidentally, are not eligible for the duty-free privilege enjoyed by legislators, judges and government top brass.

The NEA regards the powerful but unauthorised people savouring its property as predators. But it suffers from internal predators too. They are mainly the drivers who take it as their fundamental right to pilfer petrol from the official vehicles they drive. Any breakdown, real or manufactured, in the vehicles means extra dough.

The NEA spends an average of Rs. 230,000 annually, which includes drivers' salary, fuel, Mobil oil, maintenance, etc. Under the new scheme, it pays its officials Rs. 48,000 each annually as transport allowance. The net saving comes to about Rs. 14 million a year. Thus in one sweep the NEA wants to keep the internal and external predators at arm's length. Whether it will succeed, only the future can tell. But what the past and present can tell us is that predators on public resources are all around.

◆

Chapter Twenty-Three

Dirty Fluid

Nepal is totally dependent on import of oil for transportation. Around 621 million tonnes of crude oil worth $125 million were imported in 1997 from the international market. It is refined in the refinery at Barauni in northern India.

Private tankers are used to transport oil from the Indian refinery to different destinations in Nepal. The adulteration starts right from the point of origin. It is mixed with kerosene and other assorted liquids.

A tanker carries 10,000 litres of oil - petrol or diesel. On the way the tanker driver routinely illegally sells 200 to 400 litres for extra money. He makes up for it by hoodwinking the dealers by foaming techniques. Before approaching the depot, the driver uses his brake several times over to create a mass of foam in the tanker. When the dealer measures it by dipping a rod into the tanker, the oil foam easily measures up to mark.

The next round of adulteration takes place at the dealer's depot. The Nepal Oil Corporation (NOC) formally allows the dealers to mix 5% kerosene in petrol or diesel. It is done, as they say, to make up for the evaporation of oil at their end. But actually the dealers mix nothing less than 15% to 20% of kerosene with their stock.

The malpractice can be understood when one looks at it in terms of pricing. In Nepal, petrol costs Rs. 40 a litre, diesel Rs. 15 and kerosene Rs. 10. The prices are fixed by the NOC. The petrol price is kept deliberately high to subsidise the diesel. This is justified on the ground that the petrol is used primarily by the affluent class as opposed to the diesel which is used by trucks and buses used for transportation of common people and mass consumption goods.

Besides the financial cheating, oil adulteration has a debilitating effect on the automobiles. How much damage it is causing to the means of mass transportation has not been calculated. But the reason why automobiles are not functioning properly is not difficult to understand. Rising air pollution can also be attributed to this factor. The government has introduced emission tests for fourwheelers in the capital city of Kathmandu for the last couple of years. Most of the vehicles fall the test because of fuel adulteration.

In the face of public concern over the problem, the government wanted to enforce quality control on oil supply. The NOC went ahead with testing the quality of oil regularly. This measure drastically cut the illegal practice of adulterating oil with kerosene. But it did not last long. The carriers went on a nationwide strike, bringing oil supplies to a halt. In support the dealers brought the shutters down. The government had to relent to the pressure and rescinded its quality control measure. Simply stated, the oil suppliers asserted their right to cheat the people.

The matter did not end there. The NOC takes pride in making profits of millions of rupees on its monopoly business. On that account, it started distributing bonuses of up to twelve months' salary to their employees. In other words, the staff got double the salary for several years. On top of that, the NOC provides comparatively better incentives to its staff in terms of medical coverage, education for children, transport allowance, house-building loans, etc. The service facilities are so attractive that political parties have turned the NOC into a recruitment centre for their cadres. The NOC is overburdened with staff. This explains why it went into the red in 1997.

When the NOC incurred losses, it raised the fuel price by more than 30%. Naturally there was a big hue and cry in the country as the hike directly affected pricing patterns across the board. The NOC tried to justify the hike by stating that following a rise in the international oil market, it was unavoidable. In fact there was no such rise in the world market. International oil prices had actually gone down in the nineties. But that did not matter for a monopoly business like the NOC.

The dirty oil has indeed created a vicious circle of sharks at the cost of the people. The efforts of the government to curb air pollution in the Kathmandu valley have been foiled. The inevitable health hazards from pollution are yet to be assessed and mechanical breakdowns of vehicles have resulted in huge national loss. The government appears hopelessly helpless, as do the citizens, in the face of dirty oil.

◆

Chapter Twenty-Four

A Big Setback

The Royal Nepal Airlines Corporation (RNAC) is the national carrier of Nepal. It operates domestic as well as international services. After several years of flights to Bangkok, Hong Kong and Singapore besides neighbouring India, Bangladesh, Pakistan and Sri Lanka, the airline added Frankfurt, London and Paris in 1988.

In 1993, the airline was enmeshed in a big controversy as it granted the General Sales Agency (GSA) European franchise to Dinesh Dhamija, a representative of a company called FARE (First Airline Representations Europe Ltd.), registered in London with a one pound investment. It is estimated that the airline lost around $4.5 million in this deal.

The issue of commission paid to officials by Dhamija raised a public uproar. The Public Accounts Committee of parliament ordered a formal investigation into the case. In its report, it pointed out that the terms of contract weighed heavily in favour of the agent.

Firstly, the airline granted an unusual 27% commission on sales of tickets to this company in contrast to the normal practice of allowing only a 12% commission, the rate paid to three general sales agents representing RNAC in Germany, Britain and France before this Dhamija deal.

Secondly, it agreed to issue 500 free tickets to FARE annually for business promotion, an extraordinary favour by any standards. The agent could use these executive class tickets in any way he liked. The airline had no say.

Thirdly, the airline also agreed to grant 10% extra 'incentive' commission in addition to the 27% already granted if the business went over $12 million. This was something unprecedented in the history of the airline.

Fourthly, normally a credit period of fifteen days was given to settle the accounts in normal transactions. But in the case of FARE, the period to do so was extended to fortyfive days.

Fifthly, normally the RNAC asks for a bank guarantee of $100 or $50 in cash per ticket given to the agents. But in this particular case, the rate was reduced to $20 and $13.33. Similarly, cargo shipments, unlike similar deals with other agencies, needed no financial guarantee from FARE. In case of loss of airway bills, it was the airline which would lose.

The investigation discovered that the deal was full of problems. The draft of the contract, which was heavily in favour of the agent, was believed to have been prepared by the agent himself. When the Dhamija deal got stuck at the level of the board of directors, the Nepali Congress prime minister G.P. Koirala personally intervened to clinch the agreement.

Finally, after several months of haggling, the board meeting was held at the prime minister's official residence. He is quoted to have instructed the board to expedite a decision on the matter. The board members took the prime minister's intervention as a clear hint to let the deal go and they, in order to keep themselves out of what they thought was an unfair deal, passed the buck on to the managing director. The managing director, in his turn, delegated authority to sign the agreement with Dhamija to his subordinate. The Public Accounts Committee demanded immediate abrogation of the contract as it found the deal against Nepal's constitution and the rules and regulations of the airline.

After some time, the government changed hands from the Nepali Congress to the Communists. A new managing director was appointed and the contract with Dhamija was cancelled hurriedly. Dhamija went to an arbitration court as stipulated in the contract. The dispute went on for about a year and by the time the verdict on the case was about to be pronounced, the Communists were dislodged from power. The Nepali Congress came back to power in a coalition arrangement with smaller parties.

A new managing director was appointed. The airline then decided to have an out-of-court settlement with Dhamija by paying a lump sum of $1.5 million as compensation for the breach of contract. The belief is that the loot was shared by Nepal's powers that be. Without the connivance of powerful people, it would not have been possible or Dhamija alone to extract such unprecedented benefits out of the deal. The net result was that the Nepalese flag carrier not only incurred financial loss but also lost face internationally as an 'undependable' client.

◆

Chapter Twenty-Five

Setback Number Two

The Royal Nepal Airlines Corporation (RNAC) suffered yet another financial setback when it granted the General Sales Agency for Thailand to a local agency called Oriel Travels. The decision was made in 1993 when the airline itself had its own sales office in Bangkok with an annual business turnover worth 70,000,000 baht ($2.8 million).

The decision to appoint a new GSA was defended by the airline management on the grounds of more business but the fact is that Oriel Travels was cut off two years ago because it had not generated enough business for RNAC. Records showed that RNAC had saved 1.5 million baht ($60,000) within a year since snapping ties with that sales agent. The irony is the official who reported profit to the head office in Kathmandu was fired to clear the way for the shady deal in the offing. When the matter came to public notice, pertinent questions were raised.

An investigation into the deal revealed that RNAC had granted an 'extra incentive' commission up to 7% on ticket sales above 3.5 million baht ($140,000). The question was why the airline which was selling tickets worth 70 million baht by itself should appoint a new agent with extra commission of 7% on sales above 3.5 million baht? It was concluded that the decision was made under political pressure.

Only two airlines fly the Kathmandu-Bangkok route Thai Airways International (Thai) and RNAC. In 1993 Thai was charging 5,500 baht for a one-way ticket whereas the Nepalese airline had fixed the rate at 4,815 baht (685 baht less than Thai). RNAC lowered its price further down to 3,875 baht in 1994. Since the flow of traffic during these years was not decreasing there was certainly no reason to slash the fare.

Obviously the reduction was believed to have been prompted by the desire to give a higher margin of profit to the agent. Although the price was fixed at 3,875 baht, the provision did not debar the agent from selling tickets at a price equal to that charged by Thai (i.e. 5,500 baht). This resulted in a net loss of millions of baht to the airline whereas the agent gained tremendously.

The investigation ascertained the extent of loss to the airline on the basis of statistics furnished by the airline itself. The RNAC flies a 190-seat B-757 on the Kathmandu-Bangkok route. With 75% actual occupancy rate, it was estimated that the income, one-way, to the airline was $22,570 whereas the operating cost of the flight was $22,770. It meant a net loss on every flight to Bangkok. Thus the total loss to the airline operating four flights a week was about $83,200 per annum.

Is it not ironical that the Kathmandu-Bangkok route which was making a profit when RNAC was managing business by itself made a loss after the appointment of a General Sales Agent who was supposed to boost the profit margin? The terms of the contract were such that it could not possibly avoid being in the red, and that was not hidden from the management.

The calculation made by the Public Accounts Committee had it that the airline incurred a total loss of $1.1 million in one year because of this deal. On the one hand the income of the airline went down by $1 million, on the other it ended up paying its sales agent an extra commission to the tune of $100,000. This decision taken at the behest of the profit-orientated political leaders who were then in the government lost the airline quite a sum, but no legal action was initiated against them despite the fact the Public Accounts Committee made no secret of who was involved in the deal.

◆

Chapter Twenty-Six

Not For Nothing

In the seventies, when there was no freedom and democracy in Nepal, a reign of terror of sorts prevailed. Some gained notoriety by excelling in illegal activities. One of them was Bharat Gurung, an officer in the Nepalese army. Linked to the most powerful lobby of the day, he could get away with anything without being booked or so it seemed.

But over time his influence waned as the regime started to distance itself from him when reports of his widespread misdeeds became known. He was subsequently arrested and put on trial at the military court. The military court, unlike the civil court, is held in camera. The people knew what he was like and were not surprised with the military court's verdict.

Gurung was prosecuted on seven counts, earning him a twenty-year sentence in jail and a fine of several millions of rupees. He was found guilty of connivance in the attempted murder of a journalist, drug trafficking, illegal foreign exchange transactions, unauthorised possession of weapons, and gold and watch smuggling. According to the prosecution accounts, the journalist lost an eye but survived the gunshot. The prosecution established that about 1,500 bars of gold, 5,500 watches and 90 pistol bullets were found in his possession. All properties under his direct ownership and in the name of his family members and relatives were confiscated. Thus, about 128 ropanies (6.5 hectares) of prime land in different parts of Kathmandu valley was seized by the government from Gurung and his close relatives.

After some years he was granted a pardon and all his properties save a few plots of land were returned to him. The people who were not at all surprised at his arrest and prosecution as they were aware of his criminal activities, were shocked when he was released and his confiscated properties restored. The whole affair looked fishy even to an unsuspecting person.

The decision led to a public uproar which forced a parliamentary investigation into the matter. The parliamentary committee detected several improprieties on which the government's decision was based. Well, wrong decisions are not deliberately made for nothing.

The political system had changed in Nepal since Gurung's prosecution. A democratic government had been formed by the Nepali Congress led by G.P. Koirala. His cabinet took the controversial decision on the basis of the recommendations made by a committee of secretaries including the Chief Secretary of His Majesty's Government.

The recommendation for a royal pardon and return of property to Gurung was made on the basis of a technical error, as pointed out by the Supreme Court of Nepal, in the verdict of the military court. It was actually related to the 'discriminatory' term of imprisonment decreed by the military court against Gurung and one of his accomplices.

The parliamentary investigating committee declared the recommendation inappropriate which was based on a wrong interpretation of the civil court's decision. The committee said that a decision made on a wrong recommendation cannot but be wrong. It also found that there was an inexplicable delay of more than a year in the publication of the government decision in the official gazette as is customary in such cases. The Chief Secretary was specifically named for misleading the parliamentary committee.

Nevertheless the government decision was carried out without any impediment. Accordingly, all the land except a few plots and other properties including two houses confiscated by the government were duly returned to Gurung and his family members. It is estimated that the properties thus returned were worth millions of dollars. It was not for nothing that the government had taken such a decision and tried to keep it a secret for as long as possible.

◆

Chapter Twenty-Seven

Lost Losses

Nepal imports every year several thousand tonnes of chemical fertiliser. The Agriculture Input Corporation (AIC) established for this purpose is fully authorised by law to take all decisions in this regard. It procures the required volume of different types of fertiliser through open global tenders.

The fertiliser is heavily subsidised by the government because the agricultural production would go down considerably (almost by 40%) if farmers did not use it but they cannot buy it at the real market price. Every year the government incurs a net loss of Rs. 1.5 billion to Rs. 2 billion ($25 million to $33 million) on this account. It is by far the biggest subsidy given by the government in Nepal.

The AIC, although in theory an autonomous public body, is controlled by the government. The minister of agriculture is directly involved in all its major decisions. The top personnel are appointed by the government. The Secretary in the ministry of agriculture chairs the board of directors.

In 1995-1996, a coalition government of the Nepali Congress and the Rashtriya Prajatantra Party (RPP) was in place. Padma Sundar Lawati, a member of the RPP, was assigned the agriculture portfolio. He was implicated in the fertiliser procurement scandals.

Nepal has an anti-corruption body called the Commission of Investigation for Abuse of Authority (CIAA). By its very name, it is clear that it can investigate and frame charges on matters of corruption against all officials including the prime minister and his ministers. When the fertiliser case hotted up in the press and on the floor of the parliament, the CIAA started investigations on the basis of complaints filed.

One of the cases was related to the import of what is called DAP fertiliser. The CIAA, after several months of investigations, framed charges against Minister for Agriculture Padma Sunder Lawati and several other highranking officials of his ministry and the AIC for directly negotiating with a private supplier at a price higher than the one quoted by another supplier.

The AIC signed a contract with the Peerless Developers Co. to import 9,000 tonnes of DAP fertiliser at $320 per tonne whereas the lowest price offered by another agency was $316.5. Thus there was over payment of $3.5 per tonne which meant a clear loss of $31,500 for the corporation.

According to CIAA charges, the minister exercised unauthorised power in this deal as the contract was signed at the behest of the minister without the knowledge, let alone the approval, of the AIC board. The document was submitted to the board for endorsement after the deal had been finalised. In this case, the chief of the AIC was also accused of tampering with information relating to the deal to favour the minister's decision.

A charge was framed and filed in the court of law. But the court dismissed it on the grounds that there was no evidence that any money had changed hands between the supplier and officials, including the minister.

In yet another case involving import of 50,000 tonnes of urea fertiliser Minister Lawati directly intervened and instructed the AIC to make a deal with an agency called Semiconductor Material Inc. of New York at $235 per tonne, whereas the original offer of the same agency was only $225-$10 less. Thus the AIC would have to pay $500,000 more than the amount originally quoted.

The deal was also found to be suspicious on the deposition of the performance bond. According to AIC general rules, the supplier is supposed to deposit 5% of the total amount of the deal as a guarantee for the supply of fertiliser. In case of failure to do so on the part of the supplier, the deposit is forfeited to the AIC. If the deal is accomplished as stipulated in the contract, the deposit money is duly returned to the supplier.

However, in this case, the contractor deposited only $146,875 whereas 5% of the total amount of the deal ($11,750,000) would come to $587,500. In other words, the performance deposit was $440,625 less than the required amount.

According to CIAA calculations, the total loss to the AIC from this deal amounted to $940,625. It thus framed a formal charge and filed it with the court, asking for redemption of this amount from the culprits, i.e. the minister and officials responsible for the decision.

In this case also, the minister was charged with abusing his authority and causing a huge loss to a public sector corporation. While the case was pending in the court, the AIC cancelled the whole deal by seizing the deposit money put up by the supplier agency saying the supply was not made on time. The CIAA lost the case.

In the third scandal, an agreement was reached between the AIC and the supplier, G. Premji Trading Co., for 10,000 tonnes of urea fertiliser in 1995 at $229.46 per tonne. The agency supplied only 6,300 tonnes.

Under such situations the performance bond is claimed by the AIC. But, on the contrary, the AIC management released the bond money of $229,460 with the tacit consent of the minister. The minister was charged with dereliction of duty. A case was framed against the minister and the managers of the AIC for causing a loss of $229,460 to the organisation and filed in the court of law requesting reimbursement of this amount to the organisation. The case was dismissed by the court on the same grounds as in the previous cases.

◆

Chapter Twenty-Eight

Rich Richer, Poor Poorer

The economic policy of Nepal loudly declares a war against poverty, but in reality it has made the poor poorer and the rich richer. The banking sector which has a vital role to play in economic development is heavily tilted in favour of the rich.

A banking survey in Nepal has established that 80% of bank investment has been monopolised by some 200 families. They are the leading industrialists and businessmen. This select group has bagged Rs. 57 billion out of the total investment of Rs. 71 billion.

The industrialists alone have borrowed Rs. 43 billion (60% of the total) from the commercial banks in the form of fixed and working capital. But they have defaulted in repayment schedules to the tune of Rs. 18 billion, almost 42% of the total loan. Big industrialists are the biggest defaulters. However, because of their dubiously established influence on the government, they are not punished. It is the smaller businesses which often get their assets auctioned or confiscated.

According to the survey, there are twenty-five business houses in Nepal which have borrowed Rs. 30 billion (40% of the total banking investment). They too have defaulted.

The number of industrialists and businessmen who have borrowed money ranging from Rs. 50 million to Rs. 250 million is 125. Most of them get the loan approved by the banks on their 'credit worthmiess'. They do not have to present any collateral as other borrowers do.

It is a common practice for this group of people to inflate the cost of their enterprises for more cash. Since the enterprises are overvalued they normally fail to clear the debts. In the final count, it is the banks which lose, not the unscrupulous borrowers. One industrialist fabricated a project in order to borrow from a bank to pay back the interests accrued to him on other outstanding loans.

Whether industry and commerce prosper or not is a different matter, but the ones who run it do. They have mastered the tricks of the trade. They succeed in hoodwinking the lenders because of the relationship they have, nurtured over the years with powerful politicians.

How callously the banking sector has acted hurting the interests of the poor, is evident from yet another instance. Nepal Rashtra Bank (the central bank of Nepal), with a professed aim of involving the banking sector in poverty alleviation programmes, has made it obligatory for all the commercial banks to disburse 1% to 5% of their investment as credit to the poor and deprived members of society.

The commercial banks are not supposed in this case to ask for collateral guarantees as is the common practice. It was quite a fair deal as the poor generally have no property to give as collateral. There is a limit though of Rs. 15,000 (about $300).

If the commercial banks are found disregarding this directive, they are penalised. The central bank makes them pay fines equivalent to the interest on the amount not disbursed to the poor on demand. Most of the commercial banks established with foreign collaboration have no branches in the villages. They are mostly confined to the capital valley of Kathmandu. Only a few banks have opened branches in towns like Biratnagar and Pokhara. So this special credit facility given to the poor is often not executed.

The commercial banks are more than pleased to pay the fines rather than involving themselves in deals with the deprived class of society. In 1996 the Nepal Rashtra Bank received Rs. 5.2 million as fines from different commercial banks of Nepal. The biggest payer of fines was Nepal Arab Bank (about 75%). The central bank of course made some money out of the regulation, but the real target group, i.e. the poor, remained deprived.

◆

Chapter Twenty-Nine

Welfare Goes to Waste

Over the last fifty years of planned development, Nepal set up a number of public institutions ostensibly to deliver goods and services to the people. In the process, the government participated directly in industry, trade, banking, airlines and public utilities like drinking water, telephone, electricity and transportation.

By 1997, the number of state-sponsored organisations reached thirty-eight. At one point the number had gone up to forty-five. In the nineties when privatisation became the buzzword, the government sold some seven such organisations to private bidders. The deals were far from clear. Not only were the fixed and immovable assets sold cheap, but politicians in the decision-making bracket reportedly received hefty kickbacks.

All public sector organisations are placed under the direct managerial and financial control of the government. The members of the board including the executive heads are appointed by the government. The financial supervision comes under the jurisdiction of the auditor general. In other words, these organisations are answerable to the Public Accounts Committee of the Nepalese parliament.

The Auditor General's Office reported that in 1997 only six out of the thirty-eight state-owned organisations had their books checked by it, meaning that most of these organisations had not had their accounts audited for several years. That is to say, many of them were deep in administrative and financial mismanagement. When so much fiscal indiscipline exists, one can imagine the extent of the damage done to the national economy.

There are some services subsidised by the government in the name of public welfare and basic need fulfilment But there are others which are supposed to compete in the free market, make profit and pay taxes to the government on par with their counterparts in the private sector. In 1996, the auditor general found twenty-two out of the thirty-eight organisations adhering to routine auditing but defaulting in tax payment to the tune of Rs. 1,240 million ($20 million).

The report also pointed out that sixteen organisations were in dire straits, incurring heavy losses. As much as Rs. 320 million, which is 68% of their equity capital, was lost. The reasons for such losses are not difficult to understand. Incompetence and irresponsibility of the managers can be blamed for the damage.

But when the matter came up for debate at the Public Accounts Committee, the public corporations held excessive official interference responsible for the sad state of affairs in the so-called autonomous corporations. The ministers were blamed for bloating the personnel. The charge was that ministers forced their political workers and relatives upon public undertakings, an act which led to a heavy drain on the resources on the one hand, and a rise in inefficiency and indiscipline on the other.

Nepal appears in a predicament as far as public sector undertakings are concerned. If you keep them running you are eroding the national treasury. If you close them down, you are letting the big investment already made go down the drain. If you sell them to the private sector for better management, you are in effect encouraging profiteering.

How the problem is to be dealt with for the greater benefit of the people, for which they were established in the first place, is a question of paramount importance. Sadly, while the national dilemma persists, a select few continue to live well as if nothing is wrong with the public organisations.

◆

Chapter Thirty

All's Yours

Kathmandu has a prime real estate property in the middle of the city. The total area is 194 ropanies (10 hectares). It serves as a parade ground for the army. Once considered Asia's biggest, it was open to the people with no fence and not divided into parts. Until the police and the army descended upon it, Tundikhel was where the Kathmanduites converged, sought relief and revelled.

Today, an ugly park has been carved out on the northern tip of the rectangular field. An open air theatre has been erected for civic and cultural activities. But political activists have monopolised the theatre for mass meetings and protests. An army pavilion stands for national functions meant basically for civil and military officials. The grassy ground is good for kids' soccer, adults' cricket and health-conscious early morning strollers. The Martyrs Memorial is yet another landmark in this open area. Then comes the army headquarters symbolising non-civilian power. The southern end serves as the sports stadium guarded by tall parapet walls and the infamous gate that, some years back, caused more than a hundred people to die in a stampede.

Thus the once famous Tundikhel (a playground) has lost its freedom and glory as it is now heavily fenced on all sides with cement and iron railings. Earlier, it had lost its historic character with the chopping down of an epochal tree named the *Kharikobot*, symbolising the sacrifices of the martyrs for the attainment of political freedom from the autocratic Ranas in 1951. It is no longer a centre of cultural festivities as access to its traditional openness has been substantially curtailed.

What remains, however, can still be a big asset in times of national emergencies like the earthquake which rocked and virtually flattened Kathmandu in 1933. Nepal lies in a seismic zone where catastrophes of this kind can recur. Where else will the people go if a major tremor hits the metropolis of over one million inhabitants?

The slow encroachment into this lovely open space continues unabated. In 1994, the police wanted to build a four-storey building just beside the Ranipokhari, a historic and cultural lake on the northern tip of Tundikhel. The site had a small government building which was burnt to ashes during the pro-democracy movement in 1990. A few sensible senior citizens and environmental outfits agitated against the proposed construction. They wanted to keep it as it was because the area could be used in times of natural calamities.

The police authorities did not question the logic but still defended the construction in the name of national security and integrity. What was at stake? A mosque stands just across the road and that could prove a threat to the Hindu king living not so far off. The home minister took an adamant position on this issue, mainly because he had already laid the foundation stone of the building. It was a matter of personal prestige as it were. The police did indeed complete the building but settled on only two storeys.

The army was not far behind in grabbing pieces of the prime site. The army headquarters are there, the army pavilion is there and now comes the army officers' club. A huge edifice cropped up without the municipality knowing anything about it. The democratically elected local body was too powerless to take the army to task. Finally the matter was taken up by the parliament's Public Accounts Committee.

The defence secretary was summoned by the Committee to explain why the construction was carried out without the permission of the municipality. The bureaucrat was very forthright when he argued the army needed no permission to build a utility centre. As the army needed a club house for the officers, the construction was authorised, he said. He defended the encroachment on the ground that some army plots were given to other government agencies like the Bir Hospital and the International Convention Centre in the past. Hence the army deserved replacements.

If the army and police grab land who can hope to deter them? After all, it is, as the saying goes, all yours.

◆

Chapter Thirty-One

Suitable but Neglected

Ropeway (cable railway) is one of the most suitable means of transport in a country like Nepal, two thirds of whose territory is covered by mountains. Some ten years back Nepal built a 22 km long ropeway as a precursor to other means of transport. The system was expanded to the Kathmandu Valley around 1947 from a point in the plains. Access to Kathmandu on a modern road did not exist till 1955.

For a valley like Kathmandu surrounded by 8,000 to 10,000 ft high mountains, the ropeway system is much more dependable and cost effective compared to roads which are vulnerable to the vagaries of nature. Just how insecure the roads actually are was illustrated when unprecedented floods swept away bridges on the main artery highway to Kathmandu in 1993. Transport fuel was immediately rationed, vegetables were in short supply and the prices of essentials skyrocketed as panic ran through the one million inhabitants of the valley. The ropeway originating in Hetauda, an industrial town in the Siwalik foothills of Nepal, came to the rescue of Kathmanduites. The supply of essentials was somehow maintained.

Unfortunately, the ropeway is going from bad to worse insofar as its management and performance are concerned. Established in 1963 with US assistance of Rs. 50 million, it is operating under the management of the Nepal Transport Corporation (NTC). The NTC also oversees other transport businesses in the public sector.

As of 1997, after thirty-four years in operation, the ropeway has incurred a loss of Rs. 90 million. The total length of the cable is 42 km over the mountains. The French government provided help in repairing a part of it in 1993 but that did not make it run smoothly. It has the capacity of transporting over 500 tonnes of goods a day.

Ropeways have several advantages over roads. A truck, for example, takes eight hours to negotiate the serpentine highway to Kathmandu whereas the ropeway can cover this distance in four hours. The trucks charge Rs. 500 for a tonne of merchandise whereas the ropeway charges Rs. 100 less.

Despite the lower cost, the merchants do not prefer the ropeway, for reasons of security and incidence of pilferage. The ropeway trolleys pass through a residential area where allegedly the merchandise is tampered with with impunity. Hetauda Cement Factory is the ropeway's only client. When there is no production of cement, the ropeway is virtually out of operation.

Not that the government is unaware or unconcerned about the problem. It has shown concern by instituting a study on the possibility of privatising this enterprise. But the government is far from decisive. It cannot pump in more resources to revamp the system, nor can it transfer the ownership to private parties.

It is not the business prospects alone which are crucial to the rapid privatisation of a government-owned enterprise. Prospects of quick invisible bucks make the difference. As reported earlier, a deal is struck only when the prospective buyers, the bureaucrats and politicians are assured of considerable profit out of the deal.

The ropeway, despite high suitability and cost effectiveness, has been pushed aside from official priority, apparently because it has not yet promised enough for private pockets. Under these circumstances, the condition of the existing ropeways cannot but deteriorate.

◆

Chapter Thirty-Two

Crumbs Only

Nepal produces innumerable herbs for the global market. This is because Nepal is a treasure house of medicinal plants. A variety of herbs are harvested in the far-flung mountains and carried across continents to manufacture some of the leading drugs for cancer, arrhythmia, diabetes, blood disorders and a host of other ailments. The herbal trade is worth millions of dollars. But what the poor Nepalese peasants who collect the herbs get are crumbs nothing more.

For example, *jatamasi* is a valuable herb used in preparing ayurvedic and allopathic tonics and drugs to serve as antiseptics, sedatives, antidotes and aromatics. Drugs against epilepsy, hysteria and intestinal colic complaints are made of it. A farmer is paid Rs. 10 at the most for one kilogram while that quantity easily fetches Rs. 140 on the Indian market. The middleman takes the difference although he shares it with forest guards, local officials and transporters. The herb actually travels to Hong Kong, Amsterdam, Hamburg and London en route to pharmaceutical companies. How much more profit is made is anybody's guess.

Nepal's herbal wealth is based on its rich biodiversity made possible by the variety of subtropical and alpine climate and vegetation. Forest cover was once widespread in all these ecological zones, so were herbal resources. According to an estimate made by botanists, there are 7,000 species of plants in Nepal. Of them, only 700 have been identified. The rest are yet to be researched and botanically classified.

But before these plants are scientifically analysed, both for knowledge and their potential value as medicines, it is feared that this unique natural wealth will be gone. The fear emanates from wanton exploitation of rare herbs, especially in the Nepalese Himalayas.

It is astonishing that the magnitude of the herbal exploitation and trade is a closely guarded secret. The data churned out by the Department of Forests gives only a partial view of what actually transpires between the middlemen and ultimate buyers. For example, in 1996 the government realised Rs. 20.6 million from the sale of 3.2 million kg of herbal plants. But it is believed that more than the recorded volume crosses the open and porous border with India, before the consignments move towards other international destinations.

The reason for keeping it a secret are twofold. One is smuggling of the banned items. The ban was imposed to save the rare medicinal plants from becoming extinct. But the high price it warrants in India and elsewhere has helped the illegal trade to thrive. When a consignment of banned items was raided in a border town of Nepal, the agent got it released by bribing the chief officer (Rs. 30,000), the police (Rs. 12,000) and the customs officer (Rs. 10,000).

The second reason is to conceal the profit made. Although the herbs are exported to different countries in Europe, the major part goes through and to India. It is the Indian merchants who exercise tight control over Nepalese herbs. In India itself, tile value of herbal medicines is estimated at Indian Rs. 8 billion per annum. Nepal consumes Rs. 1.5 billion worth of herbal medicine a year. Most of them come from India. The herbal medicines imported from India are made of the raw herbs supplied by Nepal. The government-owned pharmaceutical firm in Nepal supplies only 1% of the total demand for herbal medicines.

Some of the herbs which are used by Nepal's pharmacists are procured from Indian suppliers who in fact had them from Nepal. In this way, a large margin of profit goes to the Indian dealers.

It is again a myth that Nepal can be rich financially by trading in its rich herbal products, even though the traditional herbal trade is being boosted by modern transport systems and increasing demand from the multinationals who are searching for healing compounds for profit. ◆

Chapter Thirty-Three

A Bridge for Pride

Nepalese rivers are traditionally negotiated by native canoes carved out of a single tree. Canoes are still in use where the river current is not too swift. Rivers are generally wild and unnegotiable when they pass over deep mountain gorges. During the monsoon, they get all the more violent. The only way out is a suspension bridge. Since modern roads are still a far cry in many parts of Nepal, the suspension bridge is a vital means of movement for the people of Nepal.

The Nepalese used to build such bridges using traditional technology. Baglung district is famous for reviving this cost-effective art on a massive scale. However, when foreign aid started flowing into Nepal, many people decided to go for prefabricated bridges, ruthlessly discarding the indigenous technology. Foreign or indigenous, the suspension bridge is very useful for the rural folks and foreign trekkers alike.

In 1980, a bridge was proposed to cross the Madi river. This river cuts the Kathmandu-Pokhara highway in half. However, to go to the northern part of the highway, the people of Lamjung and Gorkha had to take the village trails. The more difficult journey was to negotiate the Madi river in a canoe. Loss of lives and property was a common occurrence. Hence the public demand for a suspension bridge.

The government agreed to build one with Swiss aid. A team of surveyors was sent to select the site where the bridge could be constructed. The crossing point was not considered appropriate because it called for a relatively long bridge. So the team identified a site, some ten minutes' walk to the north. The rocky ground was good for the bridge's foundation and the span would be shorter.

But the site was opposed by one powerful local politico. He wanted the bridge at Sisaghat, about two kilometres south of the crossing point site. The technicians protested on the grounds that both the banks of the river were extremely fragile. Besides, the traditional trail would have to be diverted by two to four kilometres, an action that would inconvenience the villagers. Since the local leader had the clout, he pressurised the government into getting his preference through. The technicians were changed and a Swiss engineer took over in redesigning the bridge at Sisaghat.

The bridge was inaugurated with a fanfare. But the cost had gone up by at least four times compared to the cost of the bridge proposed by the Nepalese technicians at a different site. Over the period, the cost factor became secondary. The primary focus was on the use of the bridge. The villagers do not use it because they have to detour a couple of kilometres in order to arrive there.

The bridge at Sisaghat still stands as a symbol of the false pride of a paranoid politician. It is out of sight and therefore out of mind of the people for whom it was built in the first place. They still take the trail built by their forefathers and they cross the Madi river in a canoe. The Swiss bridge still stands on the sandy beaches of Madi serving no purpose whatsoever.

◆

Chapter Thirty-Four

Pay for Attendance, 'Overtime' for Work

Nepal's first university, named after King Tribhuwan for his perceived love for democracy and his humane disposition, is more a seat of largesse than learning. In operation for almost forty years, it is better known today for its easygoing attitude than discipline. This is evident from the wages the teachers get for signing the attendance register and 'overtime' for taking class.

In Nepal's educational system, teachers taking class for about an hour is by far the most important feature of academic life. The rate of negligence on the teachers' part is astoundmig. First of all, the teachers have no adequate workload. For three periods daily, there are eleven teachers in one department. Going by that ratio, there is about one class per teacher per week.

The university has a standing rule that says a teacher in the intermediate level must take twenty-one classes per week, at the graduate level eighteen classes and at the post-graduate level fifteen classes. A teacher is entitled to an extra allowance if he takes additional classes. The university has no records of the teachers' work except the details of the 'overtime' paid to them for extra hours put in by them. Some of the campuses excel in paying extra money to the teachers for work on public and annual holidays and student strikes.

The university serves as the first and last outpost for job hunters. Teachers can keep their job for an interminable period. Many teachers, after having obtained a permanent status, move out to private consultancy firms, government and non-governmental sectors. When they have nothing better to do they come to the university, just to stay put and be on the lookout for a better opportunity.

The university has provided residential facilities to its teachers at a very nominal price. Even that nominal rent is not taken from them. They are provided with free utilities which can otherwise be quite costly in today's Nepal. When the teachers go on long-term training abroad they keep the house under lock and key. The teachers also borrow thirty to sixty books from the university library for months without bothering to return them for other people's use. Millions of rupees worth of books are purchased but neither a record of those purchases nor any inventory is kept.

Moreover, the university is also a sanctuary of benefits. The staff claim all the facilities given to the government employees like pensions, home leave, sick leave, provident fund, etc. But they refuse to abide by the relatively stringent regulations governing the conduct of civil servants.

The 'autonomous' university is totally dependent on the government. About 95% of its resources come from the state treasury. The total budget of Tribhuwan University in 1997 was Rs. 1,350 million. The Nepalese government follows a wrong strategy of subsidising higher education at the cost of primary education. On top of that, the misuse of resources at the university is appalling. Right at the central office, the accounts are not audited. The auditor general has made very critical remarks about the financial mismanagement of the university but to no effect.

Audited accounts reveal that about Rs. 161 million had been paid as advances to individuals in one year. The registrar and the administrative chief had taken an advance of Rs. 2 million for unknown reasons with no supporting documents. The university staff were paid unauthorised 'overtime' worth some hundred of thousands of rupees out of loans from the IDRC (International Development and Research Centre [Canada]).

A World Bank loan given to improve the standard of education had been used for unauthorised purposes. A contractor had been overpaid about half a million rupees for a questionable job. Similarly, another half a million rupees had been paid to an adviser for an extension services not authorised by the terms of reference. In yet another instance, half a million rupees in excess of

the construction work actually performed was disbursed. The list
of foreign assistance to the university is pretty lengthy but longer
still is the list of misappropriation.

◆

Chapter Thirty-Five

Easy Come, Easy Go

As part of the democratic process of decentralisation, Nepal has been encouraging local bodies to shoulder more and more public responsibility. Quite contrary to that noble principle of transparency in transactions, the municipalities of Nepal engage in shady deals and dubious transactions. They collect revenues in a suspicious manner. Worse still is the way they spend the public money. The local bodies have made the octroi (duties) their main source of income for the last two decades, letting it bring in 90% of their total income.

The municipalities can levy 1% tax on all commercial goods entering an area under its jurisdiction. But they are supposed to collect the octroi directly through their own mechanism. Instead of doing so, they auction the authority out to private bidders. Since that leaves a great deal of room for manipulation by the contractors as well as the municipal authorities, the system is a breeding ground of corruption.

The Kathmandu Metropolis when it contracted out octroi collection for Rs. 700 million came under heavy public criticism. The Pokhara municipality granted the right to a contractor for Rs. 400 million. It too was subjected to public ire for not being transparent. People believe that the octroi collection far exceeds the quoted amount. If the municipalities are not capable of collecting octroi by themselves, it had better be abolished. There is no reason why the collection of resources from the public should go towards private benefit. The municipalities have turned a deaf ear to the outcry, and so has the government.

Moreover, the expense side also arouses public suspicion. The Kathmandu Metropolitan City has thirty-five wards and it provided between Rs. 11.2 million and Rs. 17.4 million each to the ward chairman to be used as a discretionary fund over a period of four years, 1992-96. The grant was deemed pocket money or a reward of sorts to municipal functionaries. At a time when the city air was stinking with solid waste splattered all over, handouts of this kind could not but offend people's sensibilities.

It is at such a juncture the octroi-paying traders demanded immediate abolition of the system. The people in general supported the demand because it was they who were ultimately made to bear the brunt of this tax. The government did not agree to abolish the tax because it would mean its financial grants to the local bodies would have to be increased. The municipalities, on their part, wanted to continue with the system for reasons not hidden from anybody.

Collection of taxes through other means is possible but is regarded as too cumbersome from the local bodies' point of view. When easy money is coming in, why bother to make it more difficult? They are therefore resisting the pressure to abolish the octroi system.

The problem went from bad to worse when the municipalities became increasingly indiscreet in the collection of octroi, irrespective of the destinations of the consignments of goods. The law provides for imposition of octroi at only one place, the final destination. But the rule is observed more in non-compliance. When the consignment passes through various municipal points, the tax is charged at every point. Non-payment can result in detention for several days.

Even on being convinced that the octroi system is encouraging the misuse of public resources, the government continues to tolerate it. On their part, the municipalities are happy with the steady supply of easy money, spend it in easy ways and more importantly, have an easy life for themselves.

◆

Chapter Thirty-Six

The Long Chain

The Timber Corporation of Nepal (TCN) was established in 1961 by the Government with the object of managing timber supply not only nationally but internationally. But after operating for over thirty-five years, its scope was restricted to local markets. The miserable situation of having to undergo losses year after year would ordinarily have made the TCN pull the shutters down. But the government wanted to give it a last lease of life by handing over to it the monopoly of logging and marketing timber in Nepal. It is still unlikely that it can be saved.

The destiny of the Timber Corporation is linked to the fundamental question of why a cubic foot of timber costs Rs. 1,100 in the market when the government charges the TCN only Rs. 200 per cubic foot. The story begins and ends with a long chain of underhand deals in the timber trade. The forest officers or the Timber Corporation, the two wholesale dealers of timber in Nepal, arbitrarily add Rs. 150 per cubic foot for themselves.

At the logging site, the timber contractor has to pay an extra charge of Rs. 10 to Rs. 15 to the district forest officer, and Rs. 15 to Rs. 20 to the departmental head or the corporation head. Some unseen sum has to be delivered to the other officials, the higher they are the greater the pay off. The total amount of these seen and unseen bribes amount to nearly Rs. 125 per cubic foot.

While in transit from the logging site to Kathmandu market, some additional expenses are incurred. In every district there are a couple of checkpoints to examine the timber consignment in order to contain illegal logging. These checkpoints are not supposed to charge any fee. But the truth is that if they are not paid from Rs. 50 to Rs. 200 per consignment, it is stopped indefinitely. In this way, one truck of logs reaching Kathmandu from, say, Jhapa in the eastern border district costs Rs. 3,500 extra.

This is the story of a hardwood, *shorea robusta*, a fast disappearing species from the forests of Nepal. It is not easily regenerated because it takes sixty to eighty years for the tree to grow for commercial use. The logs can survive, even in the open, for as long as 200 years. Nepal is a land of paradoxes. There are huge piles of such logs in western Nepal, harvested originally for rehousing the people, road construction and development works in the forested areas. But for want of an access road they remain there unused, whereas there is an acute shortage of timber in the eastern and middle sections of Nepal, a sure danger to the standing forests in those areas.

It is estimated that if bribes were eliminated from the timber deal, the price could come down by at least 40%. But nothing is being done by the government. What the government was doing was giving the monopoly market to the Timber Corporation, which is famous for innovating all kinds of irregularities in the timber trade. When the government itself patronises a corrupt agency, encouraging it to be more corrupt, no way can the people hope to get the timber at reasonable rates.

◆

Chapter Thirty-Seven

Greed Overcoming Generosity

Guthi, a traditional trust, provides a glimpse of how generous the Nepalese can indeed be. Trusts are initiated by the royals and the commoners alike for their spiritual satisfaction. In most cases land is set aside under the management of the trust to sustain religious or altruistic activities on a long-term basis. As the number of such trusts runs into thousands, the government has created the Guthi Sansthan to take care of the assets in their name. But in practice the Sansthan manages only the royal trusts and those voluntarily joining it. The land under trusts is considered a community asset.

According to Nepalese law, all land belongs to the state unless duly registered in the name of individuals or institutions. In that sense, one could argue government land too is public property. There are instances of the community using government land for collective benefit.

How greedy the Nepalese can be can be understood from cases of unauthorised encroachments into government and public land. It is particularly rankling in the urban area where the value of land is sky-rocketing. In Kathmandu, the situation is all the more glaring.

There was a time when Nepal had no shortage of land because of a smaller population. Nobody really bothered about acquiring extra land. But with the sharp increase in population, urbanisation and migration from the hills and plains to the cities, the demand for land has shot up phenomenally. Thus the encroachments into public land are not at all surprising.

Kathmandu presents the worse case scenario as, being the capital city, it attracts everyone. Until very recently, neither the government nor the national trust agency had an inventory of the public land. Traditionally and culturally, the Nepalese avoided using public land for private purpose for fear of being penalised after death. This fear had eroded though, thanks to modern education and an enhanced sense of commercialisation.

In 1993, the government instituted a high level commission to take stock of public land and to find out how much of it had been illegally encroached upon. After three years of a supposedly intensive survey, the commission submitted a not so comprehensive report. The report covered only twenty-eight of the thirty-five wards of the Kathmandu metropolis.

The commission established that out of 13,762 ropanies (700 hectares), 1,246 ropanies (63 hectares) had already been illegally encroached upon. In other words, 9% of the recognised public land has fallen prey to private greed. In terms of size, the figure might not raise alarm, but the price of this land at the current rate is estimated to be ten billion rupees.

In previous years, the kings and other feudal lords gave away land to their henchmen and cronies mostly as a reward for the services rendered or simply as a personal favour. The practice came to be known as a system of *birta*. However, the recipients had to pay the rent to the state in cash or kind. *Birta* was however abolished in 1959. It was estimated then that nearly one quarter of the whole kingdom of Nepal had been so gifted out to individuals.

The practice of royal donation of public land nevertheless continued till the end of 1970. After that, the 'donation' receded because there was very little land left for dole out. Moreover, public awareness had grown quite remarkably against this typically feudal practice.

When the pressure on land went up due to urbanisation, non-agricultural use, midustrialisation and fast population growth, the government put a ceiling on land holding in the mid-60s. A family was entitled to 25 bighas (17 hectares) in the Terai, 50 ropanies (2.5 hectares) in the Kathmandu valley and 80 ropanies (4 hectares) in the mountains. The extra land was formally seized by the government for distribution among the landless peasantry. Has that been done? The answer, unfortunately, has to be in the negative.

◆

Chapter Thirty-Eight

Goodbye to Gods

By remaining isolated till 1950, Nepal may have paid a price of sorts insofar as her modernisation is concerned. But her cultural treasures were left untouched. In came the foreigners, out went the gods. It could not have been a coincidence that as Nepal opened her doors to foreigners in 1951, she witnessed the first ever disappearance of twelve idols from Jaisideval in Kathmandu.

Before that watershed, the objects of art and culture were safe even in public. Those Western scholars like Percival Landon, Daniel Wright, Oldfield, Sylvan Levi, Kirkpatrick and Percy Brown who toured Nepal with special permission were dazzled by the beauty of the stone sculptures, bronzes, wooden works and paintings.

No less awed were other visitors for whom Kathmandu valley was an open museum splashed with icons of gods and goddesses on display. However, the appreciation received by Nepal's cultural heritage reflected in the temples, shrines, stupas and wood and terracotta pieces inspired a steady demand in the antique market of the world. The flight abroad of Nepalese gods and goddesses was inevitable.

By 1985, it was estimated that more than half of Nepal's antiques from over two thousand years was carted off in thirty years of open interaction with the outside world. An account of about two hundred stolen images of Nepal gives a visual description of how priceless pieces were vandalised and exported. Where have the beauties gone?

The Nepalese antiques are now the prize possessions of famous museums and private art collectors of the United States and Europe. In 1964, the Asia House Gallery organised a big exhibition of Nepalese antiques. In 1966, the Museum of Fine Arts based in Wanton, US, brought out a catalogue of Nepalese art pieces on display in its gallery. The Los Angeles County Museum of Arts also produced in 1985 a long catalogue of similar pieces from Nepal which permanently adorn its shelves.

Alarmed by the trend of increased theft of idols and images, the Nepalese government made official inspection of all handicrafts and souvenirs before they left the country obligatory. Although the regulations are still in place making official clearance of such goods compulsory, there are just too many chinks in the armour.

Rules say all art pieces over a hundred years old are antiques and therefore not allowed out of the country. As professionals in the Department of Archaeology are the only ones to certify the antiquity of such pieces, a lot of room is left for personal discretion. Under such an open arrangement, the chances of oversight are rather high. When dishonesty creeps in, rare cultural treasures of the country are the casualties.

Most often it was officially admitted that for want of competent professionals, art pieces meant for export are examined by the quacks which widens the margin for human error. There is moreover a long open border with India through which the antique smuggling can be carried out with no difficulty. On occasions the Indian authorities recover the stolen antiques of Nepal in transit but the recovered ones are never restored to Nepal.

Despite the precautionary measures taken by the government and enhanced public awareness of the issue, the problem is far from effectively dealt with. It is believed that there is a gang of foreigners aided and abetted by the natives that specialises in lifting and transporting ancient art pieces of Nepal for huge financial gains. In fact, big names of Nepal have often been named in this nefarious trade. Who dare catch them? Smaller fry are the ones who get caught.

◆

Chapter Thirty-Nine

What Does God Want?

The King of Nepal, being a Hindu by faith, invokes the power of Lord Pashupatinath, the God of Gods to bless the people of Nepal in every public exhortation. The most sacred temple of all is located on the bank of the Bagmati river in Kathmandu. The temple has been kept off-limits for non-Hindus.

In pre-1950 Nepal, the Indian Hindus who came on pilgrimage to this famous temple were allowed entry only during the festival of *Shivratri*, the Night of Lord Shiva. There is no such restriction today for Indians who need no visa to visit Nepal.

The Pashupatinath temple, being one of the top destinations for Hindu devotees, naturally attracts a large number of visitors both from within Nepal and India all through the year. The crowd swells specially during the *Shivratri* festival which usually takes place in February. 100,000 pilgrims converge in Kathmandu on this occasion.

For many, it is a lifetime dream fulfilled and they want to express their happiness by making handsome offering to the deity. As Lord Shiva (Pashupatinath) is believed the creator, sustainer and destroyer of all living beings in the world, the devotees come to the temple to pray for good health, happiness and prosperity. Offerings in terms of cash, kind and valuables are made to placate him.

Whether the god is really pleased with these offerings is something which cannot be easily verified. But the priests are certainly very pleased with what is offered. The priests at Pashupatinath temple are from Karnataka state of India and have been 'monopolising' Nepal's most revered deity for over the last

300 years, thanks to a decree issued by the then king, Pratap Malla. These priests not only control access to the god but also oversee the flow, both ways, of all the offerings made to the Lord by the hundreds of thousands of devotees.

According to a conservative estimate, the average daily income of the temple is easily above Rs. 10,000, which works out to be Rs. 3.6 million a year. But some estimate that Rs. 20 to Rs. 30 million is made annually. The temple made nearly Rs. 10 million during the *Shivratri* festival in 1998. In the official records the priests have shown only Rs. 600.

The 'white' money earned by the temple goes to a trust set up centuries ago while the 'black' variety is siphoned off by the priests to their homeland for investment in hotels and other lucrative businesses. This they do out of loyalty to their place of origin, India.

The priests have come under public fire from time to time for 'personalising' public donations to Pashupatinath. They have also been charged with misusing the immovable assets of the temple. Allegedly the priests have leased out the land belonging to temple for 100 to 150 years against payment of large sums of money.

Several official and unofficial attempts have been made to bring them to book but all in vain. One big reason why they continue to enjoy immunity is apparently the reluctance on the part of the Nepalese king to offend the high priests. How the god himself feels about this situation is of course anybody's guess. But how the people are reacting to it is anything but pleasant. Can such a flagrant misuse of authority and resources be tolerated right under the god's nose?

The irony of the whole situation lies in the fact that there is a body called the Pashupati Development Trust (PDT) headed by no less a person than the Queen of Nepal herself. This trust is supposed to restore or conserve the ancient monuments and scriptures, and manage the forest, drainage and other assets of Pashupati Temple. But the PDT has failed to deliver primarily for lack of funds. Resources have to come from the government which itself is financially hard pressed to meet the PDT's demand for additional funds. Isn't it ironic that the resources generated by the temple go into the hands of the priests and then to India while so much still needs to be done to preserve and upgrade Nepal's premier cultural heritage? Calls to make all donations accountable are gaining momentum. The government has already passed legislation governing the use of money like some famous temples in southern India. The temple of Tirupati of India is said to have an annual income of Rs. 8 billion which is fully accounted for and used not only in managing the temple but also funding several programmes in the education, health, and public welfare sectors.

Whether the god's money will ever be used in Nepal for starving beggars and old people living in the temple's neighbourhood and managing the whole of Pashupati area is yet to be seen. What is however evident is that even the god's house is not free from modern sins - misuse of authority and resources in particular. What does God want? Does he want change? The devotees in Nepal are waiting to be told, one way or another.

◆

PART IV

Industry, Commerce and Exploitation

Chapter Forty

A Windfall Prize

As in other developing countries, Nepal established in the 1950s a number of public enterprises in the goods and services sectors. By 1990, the number of such enterprises had gone up to forty-five. Every industry, trading agency or basic needs, social welfare and financial services was in the public sector. The government is still the biggest investor, biggest industrialist, biggest trader, and biggest service deliverer in Nepal. For over four decades the government took immense pride in establishing newer and newer enterprises. But the empire grew so big that it became unmanageable, hence the fast deterioration in efficiency and performance levels.

After the downfall of Soviet communism, and as the global wave of socialist principles suffered a great setback, Nepal too was shaken by the wind of free enterprise. The political changeover in 1990 from a dictatorial regime to a democratic one marked the privatisation of the public enterprises as a means to relieve the government from a never-ending financial liability on the one hand, and to infuse efficiency and dynamism in governance on the other.

Until that time, the government had already invested Rs. 6 billion and granted credit of over Rs. 15 billion to all these assorted organisations. No return was forthcoming as these enterprises had already incurred a huge loss of Rs. 240 million in 1990. The loss soared to Rs. 1.8 billion in 1991. The government endlessly bearing the financial burden was out of the question. These organisations reported only 52% capacity utilisation.

With the liberalisation trend sweeping through the Asian economies, including neighbouring India, the Nepalese government decided to sell off some industries. Necessary formalities were indeed completed by constituting committees to suggest the sale of what were identified as 'sick' industries. Two of the industries thus identified were the Bansbari Leather Shoe Factory and the Harishiddhi Bricks and Tile Factory.

The Bansbari Leather Factory, built with Chinese assistance, was put on sale in 1991. It had at that time a business turnover of around Rs. 15.5 million with a processing capacity of 17.4 million square feet of leather and a production capacity of 15.5 million pairs of shoes. It was built on a prime location on the periphery of Kathmandu city. The factory was sold out to a businessman who, according to the terms of agreement, was to shift the factory to another location in Hetauda, outside the Kathmandu valley. Until that point, there was no noticeable problem.

After some time another shoe factory was established with government investment worth Rs. 1 million. The equity was against the 10 ropanies (0.5 hectares) of land in which the leather factory was originally located. The land was officially valued at Rs. 100,000 per ropani. The then prevailing market price of the land was conservatively estimated at Rs. 3,000,000 per ropani. So the total value of the land was worth Rs. 30 million but the official evaluation established it at only Rs. 1 million, some thirty times less than the going rate.

The drastic undervaluation of the public land could not be effected by the decision makers and the businessmen without some sort of hand-in-glove collaboration. The reason why it was so done did not take much time to reveal itself. Both the parties gained as the country lost.

After more time, the shoe company was liquidated. The government lost its investment. However the land went into the hands of the private investors who held majority shares in the company. The profit margin from owning the land was more than enough.

This is cited as an example of how a public property is callously manipulated for private gain. As far as the policy of the privatisation of public enterprises is concerned, not much fuss is made. But when in the name of a correct policy enormous wrong is committed, the people have every reason to be alarmed. This windfall prize permitted by the government to an individual entrepreneur has served to throw a damper on the privatisation process of other public enterprises.

◆

Chapter Forty-One

The Hidden Gain

The privatisation process was found at fault in yet another case of turning a public property into a private one, arousing suspicion of clandestine deals to benefit individuals against the interest of the country. It is this kind of action that pushed privatisation on to the back burner, despite official commitment of the government, be it leftist, rightist or centrist.

One of the priority industries slated for privatisation was the Harishiddhi Brick and Tile Factory, built by the Chinese as 'a friendly gift' to Nepal before China opted for Deng's four modernisations. The factory was sold out to a group of private entrepreneurs at a price of Rs. 186.5 million.

The promoters held 61% of the shares, the factory staff 10% and the public 29%. It was obvious that the promoters acquired control of the factory.

The government was partly paid from Rs. 60 million collected from the public and the staff. The major portion was covered through loans from various banks 'in Nepal.

The loans amounting to Rs. 148.9 million were drawn from mostly the government-controlled agencies like the Nepal Industrial Development Corporation, Rashtriya Banijya Bank, Nepal Bank, Agriculture Development Bank and Employees' Provident Fund.

Thus the new owners of the factory raised Rs. 208.9 million from sale of shares and loans against the shares of the factory. On a plain and simple calculation, they had a saving of Rs. 22.4 million after they cleared the government debt on the deal of Rs. 186.5 million. So if the factory closed down for any reason, they stood to gain a cool Rs. 22.4 million in cash and the vast chunk of land over which the factory was built. The land itself is worth millions of rupees.

The factory owns about 450 ropanies (22.8 hectares) of land. The government purchased it a few decades ago at Rs. 600 per ropani for the factory from the farmers who were assured that they would be benefiting from the project. Now the land belongs to the factory.

The price of land in this area is now around Rs. 100,000 per ropani. If the owners of the factory sell just the land they would get Rs. 45,000,000. More than anything else, the land is the prize attraction for the new owners. The development of the factory in the private sector was of little consequence to the owners who were more for fast money than the slow yield from the tedious operation of the factory.

The new owners in fact planned to sell the land immediately after finalising the transfer of factory ownership from the public to the private sector. But before they could do so, the government was awoken by the villagers with a protest against the planned sale of land which the government had procured at a throw-away price from them. Immediately the government put a moratorium on the sale of the land belonging to the factory, fearing that the loans which the public financial agencies had extended to the factory would not be realised from the new owners.

This is cited as an instance of how a public-owned property including land is handed over to the private individuals for personal benefit. Even if the factory goes bankrupt, the new investors stand to make about Rs. 45 million from the land sale. It is the government-owned financial agencies who will stand to lose if the factory closes down. For the new entrepreneurs, the factory is an investment that yields them hidden profit.

◆

Chapter Forty-Two

Inbuilt Profit

Nepal is not well suited to industrialisation for reasons ranging from geographic location and landlockedness to scarcity of minerals and lack of trained manpower. This is evident from the slow industrial growth of the country despite continuous efforts on the part of the government. The Eighth Plan of Nepal (1992-1997) admits that the industrial development remained at a rudimentary stage, gaining no momentum. Thus the contribution of the industrial sector to the GDP of Nepal was only about 5%, providing employment to about 2% of the total labour force. The Plan also took cognisance of the fact that even if the number of industries had increased, the real production had not.

That however does not mean that the industrialists are losing anything. Industrialists in Nepal are so smart that they make profit before their industries actually go into operation. This 'inbuilt' profit is made possible by financial institutions which lend money to establish industries. Under a well-manipulated scheme, the project estimates are inflated so much that the establishment of the industry leaves a large margin of cash for those involved in the not so unfamiliar racket.

Even if the estimate is based and presented correctly as per the prevailing market price of the new equipment, the cash benefit is derived by requisitioning old equipment at a much cheaper price. The margin of cash savings from such a deal is adequate to pay all the unscrupulous officials and personnel involved in the deal.

A case can be cited from the establishment of a sugar plant in the private sector. This sugar plant with a capacity of 2500 tonnes production per annum was originally estimated to cost Rs. 540 million based on the standard market price of the new machinery. However over a short period of time it was hiked to Rs. 600 million, for no convincing reason.

At the original rate, the industry would have attained a break-even point utilising 70% of its capacity. But the increased cost would bring this break-even point only if the plant ran at 90% of its capacity. In other words, the profitability chances of the industry were considerably lessened. That indeed affected the repayment period of the total loan and investment on the industry. Originally, it could pay back the investment within five years but the higher cost prolonged it to seven years.

The sugar plant finally cost Rs. 658 million instead of the original Rs. 540 million, excluding the working capital, and would normally be denied loans from the financial agencies. The return on investment would go down from 30% to 20% in the fifth year of its operation. That meant a decrease of 30% in the annual rate of return on investment. In other words, the industry did not appear promising within a reasonable time frame.

But the industry was actually commissioned. The government-owned financial agencies put in the money despite its questionable economic viability. Institutionally, as the industry appeared unprofitable, the finance companies did not appear so convinced of its feasibility. But nevertheless the deal was clinched.

The secret of this venture lay in the benefits the industrialists and the loan-sanctioning authorities stood to make together from going ahead with it. It was made possible by hiking the investment cost. On top of it, an old set of machinery was installed, contrary to the provision made in the feasibility report. That radically boosted the immediate profit margin.

Out of the total allocated cost of Rs. 600 million for the machinery, the management actually spent only Rs. 80 million. The remaining amount of Rs. 520 million got transformed into invisible profit of the visible industry. If ever the industry goes bankrupt, it is the government-owned financiers who will lose. The private industrialist has already made a huge profit out of it. Whether the plant runs or collapses is now a matter of secondary importance to him. Industrialists who are adept in making 'inbuilt' profit out of new ventures are not serious about industrialisation. Why should they be? ◆

Chapter Forty-three

A Milking Cow

The Biratnagar Jute Mill established in 1935 was the first industry in Nepal. Its historic importance is also identified with the freedom movement of Nepal against the one-family rule of the Ranas. The workers of this industry launched the first ever strike of Nepal in 1947. Some leaders of this agitation later became prime ministers. Over fifty years of its existence and operation it has served as a milking cow for its government-controlled management.

With about 3,000 workers and officers in this oldest industry, the government which holds the majority share did not dare close it down despite recurrent losses. The major commercial banks of Nepal as well as the Manila-based Asian Development Bank have extended loans to streamline and upgrade this industry. But when the liability went up to Rs. 500 million with no sign of redemption, the government decided to hand its management to a private company in the hope of shielding it from certain death.

The mill was initially running at a profit. At that stage it was one of the most reliable sources of foreign currency. Where there is money there is corruption. Sooner rather than later the mill became a hotbed of resource misuse and mismanagement. Consequently the physical and financial conditions of the factory went from bad to worse. Thus the government had to lease it out for improved management.

Even the leasing-out process was dubiously executed. Three bidders responded to the open tender. Bidder A was selected and summoned to sign the management contract. But before the signing was done, the government changed its mind and awarded the contract to bidder B. Consequently, bidder A complained to the anti- corruption body which is still looking into the matter.

Meanwhile, bidder B took charge of the industry and started to run it. However no sooner was the ink on the contract dry than his intentions became crystal clear. He too meant to milk the cow. According to the terms of the contract, the industry was entitled to 80% of the profits with the remaining 20% going to the management contractor. But in practice it was the other way round.

The new management procured about 200,000 maunds (74,640 quintals) of raw jute at an inflated price causing a net book loss of Rs. 9 million to the factory. But the money thus made went straight to private pockets. On the import of spare parts, the management drastically under-invoiced the price to evade the customs duty but it over-invoiced the price by 200% in the factory book. The difference of Rs. 10 million thus generated from the shady deals also went to the new management in its very first year.

The manager withheld payment of Rs. 5 million due to the electricity authority with the clear objective of swindling the amount in case his management contract was terminated. He borrowed Rs. 33 million from a commercial bank using jute products as a collateral. But he used the amount not to promote the jute business but to clear his personal debts. He could do it only with connivance of the chairman who was a government nominee. He also managed to insert a clause in the contract saying that the industry would bear the expenses of spare parts until the mill attained the production level of forty-two tonnes per day, its optimum capacity. The fact of the matter was that it was never supposed to achieve its optimum production capacity.

According to the original contract, the manager was supposed to invest Rs. 50 million in the industry excluding a deposit of Rs. 5 million. But he did not do so. Instead he put Rs. 8 million into the industry as a personal loan from him. One year into the new management, he bagged Rs. 60 million and claimed a further Rs. 15 million from the industry. He was in a hurry to make the most of the opportunity and was ready to go to any extent to milk the cow. The tacit consent of his bosses under the principle of shared benefits was not so difficult to get.

◆

Chapter Forty-Four

Foreign Orientation

Nepal is not very rich in mineral resources, primarily because Nepal is geologically made of young mountains. However there are firm deposits of some minerals which are considered commercially viable. Coal is one of them. Coal is found in the western region of Nepal, especially in the district of Dang.

The Department of Mines regulates all mining activities in Nepal. Seven licensed companies extract coal on a small scale. The annual total production is currently estimated at 15,000 tonnes whereas the current demand in the Nepalese market for coal is around 40,000. In other words, there is a ready market for the local coal but thanks to the personal interests of few officials the mining operation faces a premature death. The coal industry has provided jobs to about 1,000 poor people. The employment rate could double but for the reluctance on the part of the Nepalese industries to use the local product in favour of foreign products.

The primary reason why the Nepalese coal cannot find a proper market is that the cement, brick and paper industries of Nepal do not use local coal. Instead they import coal worth Rs. 250 million ($4 million) from India and Bhutan. The government has established a company called Coal Limited to import and distribute coal to industries in Nepal.

Is there something wrong with the Nepalese coal that the local industries don't use it? The industrialists claim that the locally produced coal is better than the imported variety. But the government officials involved in the import company allege that the sulphur content in the local coal is too high (2.5%). The industrialists don't agree.

The producers claim that the sulphur content is less than 1%, which is technically acceptable to the industries. The government company however does not encourage the local producers, primarily because of the personal gain the officials derive from the import deals.

The locally produced coal is naturally cheaper than the imported coal. It is available at Rs. 1,500 per tonne at the production site. The transportation cost may make it double at the delivery points but it will still be 50% cheaper than the imported coal, which costs Rs. 6,000 per tonne. But the pricing logic would not have the official dealers change their preference for foreign products. From their point of view, the higher the cost, the greater the commission.

The coal producers have to face yet another hassle. They have to pay a certain amount of royalty to the Department of Mines for extraction of coal. But there is yet another claimant to this royalty, i.e. the Department of Forests. The coal producers just cannot pay two agencies out of the meagre income they make. The net result is endless hindrance to the production schedule itself. On top of that, if the coal mine happens to be on a farm the producers have to pay compensation to the farmers as well.

There is no question that employment opportunities have been created in areas where coal has been discovered. Besides Dang, coal has been found in the Piuthan, Salyan, and Rolpa districts. But instead of encouraging the coal industry to grow, all kinds of disincentives are made to militate against it. It will not be at all surprising if the coal industry in Nepal dies on account of the sheer callousness of the government authorities.

Where there are no prospects for mining development in Nepal there is no room for regret. But where there are prospects and it is not properly encouraged to develop, that provides not only a reason for regret but also leaves much room for suspicion and doubt about the intentions of the people responsible. Being on a small scale and using unskilled labour, the coal industry is directly benefiting the poor in the neighbourhood of the mines. But that is not something of interest, let alone priority of a government engaged in widespread corruption and malpractice.

◆

Chapter Forty-Five

Brewing Trouble

One of the biggest foreign-exchange earners of Nepal is the carpet industry in which a large number of poor people are employed. The benefits accruing from it are widely distributed. This handicraft is perhaps the only item in which Nepal can compete with other carpet exporting countries with some measure of success. However, it faces problem of serious nature.

Nepal exported woollen carpets worth more than Rs. 78 billion ($1.5 billion) in 1996, with about 80% of the carpets (Rs. 64 billion) going to Germany. In terms of volume, it amounted to over 2.6 million square meters of the product. European countries have been the main markets for the Nepalese carpet. The United States has started to buy it, and in 1996 it imported 3.3% of Nepal's carpets worth about Rs. 268 million.

In 1994, a big slump occurred in the export business when the issue of child labour rocked the Nepalese carpet industry. The slump was caused by a program on German television giving a vivid description of the exploitation of child labour in this otherwise thriving industry. Since then there has been a steady decline in the demand for carpets in Germany. However, the government devised a system whereby the carpets could be certified as child labour free before they were despatched overseas.

Child labour as such is an intricate issue having different dimensions in Nepal compared to Western countries. It is not uncommon in Nepal to use children in household chores which makes it virtually impossible to control. There is a natural demand for child labour and the supply is uninterrupted. Child labour in a sense is a direct outcome of free market forces so passionately championed by Western leaders. To dispense with child labour from this and other sectors of the economy, the whole structure of the poverty-dominated economy will have to change. But the basic character and structure of poverty is not changing because of exploitative forces in play at home and abroad. To deprive the children of an opportunity to work will be tantamount to depriving them of a steady source of sustenance.

This is not to say it is the only hindrance to the growth of the carpet industry in Nepal. In fact, it is a suitable industry for a country like Nepal where free hands for cottage industries such as carpet spinning and weaving are required. Moreover the raw materials and necessary equipment are locally available. But this industry does not seem to have smooth sailing. Anything that hampers its growth is detrimental to Nepalese interest especially those of the poor.

But that does not seem like a matter of any great concern to the importers as well as the exporters of carpet. For the importers, the dominant concern is to get rid of the stigma of child labour involvement. For the exporters, it is profit all the way. It is the exporters who are brewmig new trouble for Nepal's carpet industry.

A new dimension of trouble has come up. There is a simmering conflict between the producers and the exporters of carpets on the issue that the exporters mix Indian carpets with the Nepalese variety in export consignments. The matter came to a head when a truckload of Indian carpets was nabbed by the police at the border post. It stands as glaring evidence of the illegal import of foreign carpets for shipment overseas as Nepalese products.

The reason is the Indian carpet is cheaper by at least $10 to $25 per square metre than the Nepalese product. When the exporters send out the Indian products with a Nepalese name tag their profit margin is higher. But the Nepalese carpet manufacturers lose their market share. Moreover, Nepalese carpets can also lose their original reputation if inferior Indian ones are mixed with them. The practice may very well put an end to this industry, throwing thousands of poor Nepalese out of a job, and out of a livelihood.

◆

Chapter Forty-Six

Sell Cheap, Buy Dear

Like many developing countries, Nepal remains poor because it markets raw materials cheap but, after they are processed in some foreign land, buys the finished products dear. It sounds normal given the international trading conditions which offer an edge to industrialised countries over poor developing countries. For various reasons, processing industries cannot develop indigenously despite the abundance of raw materials. If lack of resources and expertise precludes growth of processing plants sometimes, irresponsible acts of responsible people account for sluggish progress in this sector at other times.

Of the items which Nepal exports cheap and imports dear, leather is one. It exports raw hides at throwaway prices. But it imports finished leather at a much higher price. So the government banned export of raw hides, saying anybody interested in exporting this item must undergo at least one stage of processing the raw hide in order to add value to this item.

But no sooner was it said, the order was retracted. When the real reason was sought, the officials started passing the buck from one to the other. There was no one in the government who would own up to this sudden change in policy.

Ordinarily, it is difficult to find fault with the policy of the government. The official policy statements usually attract commendation. The Eighth Plan, for example, speaks about encouraging export-oriented industries and specifies that in the field of leather goods production necessary training would be provided and that a scientifically equipped slaughterhouse would be set up. An allocation of Rs. 15 million was announced for these purposes alone. Nothing has happened to date.

The government even established what is known as The Hide Collection and Development Corporation Limited in the public sector to deal exclusively with this business. The plan was to collect and sell as many as 1.3 million pieces of hide.

The intention clearly was to process leather in a relatively large scale before it is finally exported. It had set a five-year target of processing wet blue leather of around 8.8 million square feet, crushed leather around 6 million square feet and finished leather around 5.2 million square feet. Similarly about 15 million shoes to be produced for internal use as well as export. The government would invest about Rs. 85 million from its own resources in developing leather processing plants. However, after the privatisation of a public sector shoe factory, the idea just disappeared.

Statistics show that Nepal's export of hides was on the increase. In 1995, it exported 1.7 million square feet of cattle hide worth Rs. 70 million. During this period, it also exported about 5,000 square feet of processed cattle hide worth Rs. 200,000. In other words, Nepal earned Rs. 10 per unit of raw hide whereas it received Rs. 40 per unit after processing. Similarly, it exported during the same period 8.3 million square feet of goat and sheep raw hide for Rs. 350 million.

In 1996, it exported 1.4 million square feet of raw cattle hide at Rs. 40 million whereas export of 800 square feet of processed hide earned Rs. 29,000. In other words, raw hide fetched Rs. 28 while the processed one fetched Rs. 36 per unit.

Despite such an obvious gain in the export of finished hide, the government allowed the raw hide to be exported. The reason can be explained by the amount of pressure exerted by the businessmen and the incentive the private sector offered to the officials to sabotage what appeared to be a sensible policy.

In order to save face, the government set a calendar of operation ostensibly to reduce export of raw hide and to at the same time increase the volume of processed hides from Nepal. According to the schedule, the export would be 15% of processed and 85% of unprocessed hide in 1998. In 1999, the ratio would be 30% and 70%. In 2000, it would be 50:50. After that period, it would be 75:25 for two years. Thereafter there would be a total moratorium on the export of raw hide.

Again, the whole agreement between the government and the private sector looks good on the surface. Whether it will be implemented remains very much to be seen. The government acts seriously when there is a hidden profit for its officials. National interest is secondary. National interests are negotiable but personal interests are sacrosanct and non- negotiable.

◆

Chapter Forty-Seven

The Glittering Stones

For the last thirty years, a mysterious mine has been in operation at an imposing altitude of 4,720 metres in the foothills of the famous Ganesh Himal, an attractive tourist destination. How much and what product the mine churns out is a riddle inside an enigma. The government has given a license for exploitation of lead and zinc. But the villagers believe rubies, a precious stone, are being mined. The industrialist who has taken about five square kilometres from the government maintains a stony silence. He neither confirms nor denies what the villagers are saying.

The issue is simple. If the industrialist is mining rubies which he is not authorised to do, he is defying the law. If he admits he is mining it, he may either end up losing the licence or paying higher royalties. Even the Nepalese royal palace has been dragged into this business of sharing the booty. So, the prospector keeps mum.

It is astonishing that Nepal Metal Company, which runs the high altitude mine, is a joint venture of the Nepalese government, an Indian industrial house and a prominent Nepalese businessman. The government officials who are members of the company board of directors feign ignorance about the illegal prospecting of precious stones. Because of the government participation in the venture, the officials rule out the possibility of the licence being cancelled, regardless of the allegation that a national mineral of considerable value is being exploited rather cheaply.

The company was to pay Rs. 580 million in revenue to the government over eight years, provided an access road to Somdang, near the mine site, was built by the government. On royal command, the army completed the 105 kilometre road in 1985 at a cost of Rs. 250 million. But the industry chose not to abide by the agreement. None of the government departments responsible for it one way or another has ever taken up the matter of collecting dues from the industry with any measure of seriousness.

The industry is paying only Rs. 6,000 per year to the government but is apparently spending a handsome sum in greasing the palms that count. It is making millions of rupees as is evident from the mine's uninterrupted operation for over three decades. Not that the authorities are unaware of what is going on in the alpine enterprise, but the belief is the kickbacks are at play in keeping the feathers unruffled.

According to a reliable disclosure, a 1,800 metre long main canal has been dug out in the mine. Linked to it are several 300 metre long feeder canals with a modern interior lift system. When glittering stones suggesting rubies are discovered, the engineers order all the labourers out of the workplace. The stones are then carted off to Kathmandu by helicopters. The unprocessed rubies are sold for Rs. 5,000 per carat in the Nepalese market. A professional magazine published in Hong Kong has confirmed the high quality of Nepalese rubies. There is no other mine, visible or otherwise, in Nepal from where rubies are being extracted. Does it not confirm what the villagers have all along been saying?

It is claimed that the thirty-year old mine has not produced even a quintal of lead and zinc. Moreover, a UNDP survey carried out in this area had found the lead and zinc deposits not at all commercially viable. But the continued operation of the mine and the allegedly clandestine way the products are moved out of the site give credence to the public suspicion that something fishy is taking place. Since the people have no authentic evidence to prove their point at a court of law, the plunder of national wealth for private gains is let go with impunity.

◆

Chapter Forty-Eight

Smoking Out

Smoking is a national pastime in Nepal. A puff is said to stimulate most Nepalese. It also symbolises adulthood. The growing generation smokes, to herald coming of age. Cigarette smoking also serves as an ice breaker in person-to-person communication in the villages. With a stick of cigarette, one can befriend a stranger, seek a favour, and even start a romance. It is an integral part of social hospitality, served generously to please the guests.

Occupying such a highly important place in Nepalese culture and social behaviour, smoking is here to stay. There are institutions which are trying to raise public awareness on the health hazards of smoking, especially its direct relationship to some of the dreadful diseases like cancer and high blood pressure. But their voice is too weak to penetrate the eardrums of the smoking fraternity.

Since the Nepalese government had no intention of discouraging smoking as a dangerous habit, it established a cigarette factory to meet the national need. The Janakpur Cigarette Factory was set up by the government in 1964 with the assistance of the now defunct Soviet Union. The factory still stands as a monument of national economic development and international co-operation.

At one time, this factory symbolised a national fight against foreign monopoly in the cigarette business. Before it came into existence, a cigarette factory in India specialising in low-grade cigarettes was meeting practically the entire needs of Nepal. The Indian factory, for example, exported to Nepal a brand called 'Bat' worth millions of rupees.

With the coming of the Janakpur factory, the Indian factory collapsed as its product was subjected to high tariffs. The Indian factory made a last ditch effort to survive by resorting to all forms of negative campaigning against the Janakpur products.

At this critical juncture the Janakpur factory counteracted by inciting a sense of nationalism. One of its advertisements said, 'If you were to die of smoking, make sure you do so smoking your native cigarettes.

As time went by, the sentimental catch of Janakpur cigarettes began to dissipate. As one of the leading public enterprises, it developed into a centre of excessive government interference - hence corruption. Consequently it went downhill both in performance and profitability. With a staff over 2200 and a turnover production worth only Rs. 1 billion, the factory landed in the red in 1995 with a net loss of Rs. 35 million. In 1996, the situation improved a little with Rs. 1 million profit. The following year a profit of Rs. 16 million was recorded.

But as the trend of political parties in power forcing their own cadres to the payroll of public organisations increased, the Janakpur factory could not possibly keep itself away from what came to be known as 'politicisation of bureaucracy and public sector organisations'. In fact, the government has already listed it for privatisation on the grounds of poor performance, mismanagement and unprofitability. Privatisation per se poses no problem except that if past experience is anything to go by, the sale of this industry also will provide an excuse for filling private pockets.

◆

Chapter Forty-Nine

Bye-Bye Dollars

A letter of credit (LC) is a normal feature in international trade. An importer opens an LC at a bank to facilitate the dispatch of consignments of goods from other countries. The LC is based on the proforma invoice the importer receives from his suppliers. Two banks figure in the deal. All international trade is operated under this arrangement.

A little aberration in this practice can cost a country millions of dollars. That is exactly what happened to Nepal in 1996 when the so- called LC scam rocked the country. To put it in simple terms, the Nepalese traders opened the LCs and the Nepalese banks made the payment in foreign exchange against payment of the equivalent amount in local currency. But the goods in question never arrived in Nepal.

The result was that the government lost the foreign exchange for nothing, not to mention the loss in terms of customs duties, taxes and other levies. The traders had drawn foreign exchange at the official rate but used it at the unofficial rate which is higher by 8% to 15%. In other words, the foreign currency facility was misused to gain profits by a handful of unscrupulous traders.

As the LC scandal hit the headlines, the government was floored. Hurriedly a five-member commission was instituted to investigate the huge scam. Six thousand letters of credit had been issued. The commission took more than four months to prepare a report on what actually had happened.

The report concluded that about $40 million had actually been extracted by means of fraud and forgery. The probe commission also estimated that the government lost almost half a billion rupees (about $10 million) in duties and other levies usually associated with imports.

The report identified as many as 145 persons who were directly involved in the scandal, 95 of whom were traders and the rest bank staff. The biggest volume of foreign exchange, $17.3 million, was flighted from the government-owned Rashtriya Banijya Bank. The Nepal State Bank of India, a Joint venture in Nepal, was responsible for $7.8 million, the Nepal-Bangladesh Bank $7.7 million, the Nepal Indosuez Bank $1.5 million, the Nepal Arab Bank $1 million, the Himalayan Bank $0.3 million and the Nepal Bank $0.2 million.

The findings of the probe triggered commotion in Nepal. The shocked parliament asked the government to act quickly against the guilty. But the then government itself was knee-deep in internal fissures. For instance, while the Finance Ministry was all for bringing the guilty to book, the Home Ministry, for mysterious reasons, was against any such move.

A special police force was mobilised to investigate but it too, once again for mysterious reasons, adopted go-slow tactics. Because of this open division in the government, many traders involved in the deal fled the country. Only nine big businessmen were taken into custody but were later released on bail ranging from $1 million to $3 million.

The government kept on dragging its feet despite pledges to penalise the guilty ones - businessmen, bank staff and customs personnel. The assistance of the attorney general is necessary before cases are brought in a court of law but his advice was solicited only to determine the merits of the cases, not to frame charges.

Meanwhile, rumour mills went overtime saying that some influential political leaders were being bribed by the accused to get off. Some traders even threatened to expose the politicians who were involved in this scam if they were convicted by the court. The government kept on putting the case on hold until the scandal lost its whole momentum. The dollars were never returned but the illegal profit reportedly got shared by all and sundry. The LC incident has now finally been hushed up, or so it seems.

◆

Chapter Fifty

The Bleeding Mountain

Nepal has a marble industry which produces no marble. But it is operating with an incredibly high margin of profit. Paradoxical as it may sound, it is nevertheless true. How something so far-fetched can occur is indeed baffling but when you see it you have no choice other than to believe what you normally would not.

The marble mine in question is located at Godavari, about 13 km south of Kathmandu. The forest spreads over the Phulchoki, the highest range adorning the fabled valley of Kathmandu. Over the years Godavari has developed as a centre for weekenders looking for rest and relaxation. There is a well-maintained botanical garden where trees planted by visiting dignitaries form part of the overall landscape. Besides, the Godavari forest is a home to some of the world's rare flora and fauna.

The importance of the Godavari forest was very well understood by the rulers of Nepal, most of whom were not educated in the modern sense of the term. Climatologists claim that Godavari holds the key to the ecological balance of the Kathmandu valley because it is the gateway to southern monsoon rains. To preserve the natural resources of this area, a Rana prime minister issued an edict saying that anyone found felling a free on Phulchoki would be beheaded on the same tree-stump. The severe warning indeed served to keep this pristine forest intact for hundreds of years.

The discovery of marble in that mountain range was a very good piece of news for the Rana rulers who admired European architecture. Prospecting of the mine was initiated in 1934 through a small company of three Rana shareholders. The company was allowed to undertake only manual digging and blasting was disallowed. But after about some thirty years, blasting was permitted under a licence given by the Department of Industry.

The Godavari Marble Industry, a brand new entity established in 1965, stepped up its exploitation activity with explosives supplied by the Ministry of Defence. Given their nature, explosives were being handled only by defence personnel. The company was bought by a new set of entrepreneurs in 1979. Forest destruction continued under the pretext of marble extraction, but the truth is that something else was being mined.

Under a new contract with the government, the industry has a right to mine marble in an area of 1.5 square miles till 2002. The contract does not specify any limit to marble production within the allocated area nor impose any restriction on exploitation of, say, stones and gravel. It is this open-ended mandate in the licence that gives a free hand to the contractors to exploit all kinds of natural assets within the allocated area.

According to official records, the industry produced on an average 205 truckloads of stone, 13 trucks of gravel and 1.5 trucks of marble. The demand for stones and gravel for construction is very high. As the source of these otherwise free gifts of nature is depleting rapidly in the bordering mountains of the Kathmandu valley, the price goes on escalating. For the factory, it was therefore more profitable to dig out stones and gravel than to produce marble.

The raw marble it takes out in small quantities is not locally used as there is no refining facility. It is sent to India for processing and sale. The Nepalese who can afford to have marble walls and floors get their supply from India or Italy.

In terms of money, the factory has a turnover of Rs. 40 million per annum. It pays a paltry royalty of Rs. 20,000 to the government annually. In addition, it pays about Rs. 800,000 as sales tax. Income tax, excise duty, export tax, etc. have been waived by the government in conformity with its policy of promoting industries in Nepal. From this calculation, it is evident that less than 2.5% of the total income generated by this factory comes to the national treasury.

The industrialist is believed not to be left in peace despite this unusually high profit margin. He is harassed and threatened by none other than the industry and forestry ministers and officials themselves each of whom wants a piece of cake. The industrialist has been obliging them with a few million every year in order to perpetuate his business interests. The government admits that the factory is overstepping the mandate and action may have to be initiated to cancel the licence. The threat is routinely used not to protect the mountain ecology, but to squeeze more and more money from the factory owner.

In 1991 and 1992, soon after the restoration of parliamentary democracy in Nepal, there was an outcry from environmental groups against wanton vandalisation of the conserved forest, the physical dangers to the nearby school and village from splinters released during blasting and the drying up of a number of natural fountains of cultural and religious value, as well as the rising threat to valuable flora and fauna. The factory fought back and succeeded in protecting its interests through underhand deals. The issue got to the court as a public litigation case but was quashed, thanks to the help lent by some leading lawyers. Thus, marble or not, the marble industry prospers with some crumbs thrown around to potential troublemakers whilst the mountains of the once pristine Godavari go on bleeding.

◆

PART V

Irrigation, Electricity and Illusions

Chapter Fifty-One

For Whom Do the Rivers Flow?

Nepal is very rich in water resources. If ever another G7 was formed on the basis of water resources, Nepal would be there. It has more than 6,000 rivers. Because of its smallness, Nepal's rivers are rather short. The combined total length comes to about 45,000 km. Only 54 rivers flow beyond the 150 km mark while the flow of 64 rivers is limited to 10 km.

Volume-wise, Nepalese rivers are very resourceful with a total average annual run-off of 7,102 cubic metres per second. It amounts to a total run-off of 224 billion cubic metres per year. To understand this in proper perspective, it works out to be a regular flow of about 1.5 million cubic metres per square kilometre of the country. Water availability per person comes to 11,200 cumecs.

The Kosi, Gandaki, Karnali and Mahakali are the major river systems of Nepal. They are snow-fed. The medium-sized rivers are the Mechi, Kankai, Kamala, Bagmati, West Rapti and Babai. Originating from the lower mountains, the flow is perennial, although reduced during dry seasons. The third category of rivers are seasonal in nature. They originate from the lowest mountains, producing fierce floods during the rainy season.

The special feature of water flow in Nepal is that the monsoon (from June to September) accounts for 73% to 78% of the total annual flow. This implies that it has to be trapped artificially to regulate the downstream flow if economic benefits are to be taken from it. In other words, it needs to be stored for constant use throughout the year. Twenty-eight sites have been identified for high-dam reservoirs capable of regulating 82.2 billion cubic metres of water, which is 48% of the total annual amount of water. The rest is not considered economically viable.

All the water flows down to India. The Nepalese rivers constitute the head reaches of the Ganges in India, contributing 41% of its total volume. But during lean periods, the supply rises to 71%, evident at Farakka near the Indo- Bangladesh border. It is in this context that the question of why Nepal and India are engaged in water politics, water economics and water diplomacy has to be understood.

For a long time, the people in Nepal have been debating the potentials of hydropower which is estimated to be 83,000 MW, of which 42,000 MW is considered techno-economically feasible. But the government is working out viable projects for not more than 25,000 MW in the foreseeable future. The irrigation potential is equally enormous - in thousands of hectares in Nepal but in millions of hectares in India.

Going by the estimate for the investment needed to maximise electricity generation from hydropower projects, Nepal needs roughly $80 billion to generate 42,000 MW. For 25,000 MW the estimated need stands at $50 billion. As Nepal's national annual budget hovers around the one billion dollar mark, exploiting water on her own is unthinkable. Hence, there is no alternative to enlisting international support, be it direct investment, grants or aid.

Nepal rushed into this area soon after the country was opened to the outside world in the 1950s. For several decades, India was the only country interested in water projects. Whatever transpired between the two countries always invariably went in favour of India. The projects stand today as monuments to Nepal's exploitation by Brother India. It was a sort of techno-political trap Nepal succumbed to as a price for Indian support for Nepal's freedom from its own Rana rulers. Then followed a period during which there was a complete stand-off between the two countries on the water issue. With the restoration of the parliamentary system in Nepal in 1991 a new beginning was made to invite not only India but other investors also to come and participate in the commercial exploitation of Nepalese water.

A lot of myths have been created whenever the issue of water development surfaces. No occasion is missed by Nepalese politicians, officials and other public figures to drive home the point that the water resource is only the resource that can make Nepal rich and prosperous. The sooner we take up water projects, the better it is for our economics.

But when the myth is exploded and the reality is known, the people tend to react with a deep sense of shock. Information plays the vital role in the tussle between myth and reality. Because of the practice of keeping every piece of information as secret as possible, anything leaked is invariably sugar-coated. However the people do realise how bitter the pill of reality is. Many a time, it is too late. Only occasionally is the deal averted. But the issue of water, power, irrigation, finance, enterprise appears again, with a vengeance, throwing the ordinary Nepalese completely off guard. What decides the fate of the so-called 'white oil' of Nepal is not the larger, sustainable and long-term interest of the people but the petty interest of a handful of decision makers.

The water wealth is there for everyone to see; who actually benefits from it is also equally visible. The people however are misled into believing that in water-exploitation lies the solution of all the problems bedevilling Nepal. The leaders know too well that it is India who is better placed to derive higher benefits. Foreign investors know this as well as we Nepalese do, but given the prospects for profit they too would like to stick their necks out.

Who has the most to gain and the most to lose is crystal clear. India, who has gained the most in the past, continues to command the same advantage today. Nepal stands to make substantially less out of her own resources, not only because of external factors alone but also because of the corruption culture of the decision makers. The third-party investors fall into the middle in terms of profit-making, without which of course they would never come to Nepal with hydropower business in mind.

◆

Chapter Fifty-Two

Traumatic Dilemma

The total economically viable hydropower production of Nepal has been estimated at 42,000 MW, of which 25,000 MW has been under active consideration. At present Nepal is producing only 300 MW. The 1996 figure showed that around 12% of the population of Nepal has access to electricity, out of which 4% live in the rural areas. The per capita consumption is 40 kW/hour in 1996, up from 34 in 1992 and 19 in 1986. It is the lowest in the world except in Cambodia.

The hydropower development does not appear to be all that easy in the context of the fact that Nepal can add only 250 MW of electricity over a period of forty years spanning over eight Five-year Plans. The major yield has been computed from the following projects.

1. Kulekhani I and II	92 MW
2. Devighat	14 MW
3. Marsyangdi	69 MW
4. Jhimruk	12 MW

It is true that small hydroelectric plants are most suitable for electricity generation and distribution to isolated villages situated in the mountainous terrain of Nepal. There are 35 such mini plants generating a total of 12 MW. The individual plants produce from 20 kW to 2,000 kW of power. In addition to these state-sponsored plants, there are two joint-venture companies of Nepalese and foreigners producing 400 kW and 600 kW of power in remote regions of Nepal. At an individual level there are 340 micro-power plants generating a total of 1,800 kW of electricity. Eight thousand families are said to be benefiting from them.

Hydroelectric power projects currently under construction are as follows:

1.	Kali Gandaki	144 MW
2.	Khimti	60 MW
3.	Bhote Koshi	36 MW
4.	Chilime	20 MW
5.	Modi	14 MW
6.	Puwa	6 MW
	Total	**280 MW**

Projects identified as feasible for implementation in the near future are:

1.	Karnali Chisapani	10,800 MW
2.	Mahakali Pancheshor	6,480 MW
3.	West Seti	750 MW
4.	Burhi Gandaki	600 MW
5.	Kali Gandaki	600 MW
6.	Arun 111	402 MW
7.	Lower Arun	350 MW
8.	Upper Arun	335 MW
9.	Upper Karnali	240 MW
10.	Sapta Gandaki	225 MW
11.	Bagmati	140 MW
12.	Kankai	60 MW
	Total	**20,982 MW**

Nepal, going by its physical size and level of economy, does not need an enormous supply of power. By no stretch of imagination, can she consume thousands of megawatts of power in the foreseeable future. Nepal's needs can be adequately met by small and medium-sized power projects, some of which are under construction and others are in the pipeline.

The obvious market for the power generated by large projects is India which is reeling under a huge power deficit. Her northern and eastern parts, for example, will need 48,500 MW and 21,300

MW respectively by 2007, a clear deficit of 20% to 30% of its needs. Moreover, the power plants in India are mostly thermal which is not environmentally friendly. There is no doubt that India can easily consume Nepal's power for an indefinite period of time.

When Enron, an American energy company, appeared with a proposal to invest in Nepal, a new dimension was added. For the first time a multinational said that export of Nepalese power need not be limited only to India, but could go to China also. A transmission line can be installed to connect Xian in China, 3,000 km away from Nepal, to facilitate a regular supply of Nepal's power to China.

Whether it is only a gimmick to fascinate Nepalese decision-makers or a plausible proposition is a million dollar question. The American company has fed the Nepalese psyche with such staggering figures of investment and return that the whole nation started dreaming. To believe or not to believe is the dilemma. The politicians, having smelt the prospect of personal gains, are all for the deal. The question of whether national interest will be served is, however, still unanswered.

◆

Chapter Fifty-Three

The Thirsty Land

Nepal is an agricultural country but two thirds of the land mass comprises mountains, leaving a relatively small space for cultivation. The total cultivated land, about 2.6 million hectares, has reached a virtual point of saturation. Of this, 1.7 million (66%) is considered irrigable. The rest, i.e. 34% of the land, has to depend on the rain gods.

Nepal has irrigation facilities for 1.06 million hectares, only 60% of the total irrigable land. The other 700,000 hectares (40%) of the irrigable land, are yet to be provided this facility.

Nepal can be divided into two parts - the Terai (plain) and the mountains. All of the land in the Terai is irrigable. In the mountains, 428,000 hectares (33%) of 1,282,000 hectares of cultivated land is irrigable. In the Terai 846,000 of its irrigable 1,338,000 hectares (63%) have already come under irrigation coverage, whereas in the mountains it is 50% (214,000 out of 428,000 hectares).

However the present situation of the irrigation system is pathetic in the sense that its efficiency is only 30% to 40% of its actual capacity. Only about 35% of all the irrigated areas get water all year round, whereas the rest (65%) get water only during the monsoon. Irrigation coverage in the Terai is 32% and in the mountains it is 40% on a year-round basis. The rest of the region is solely dependent on seasonal supplies.

At present, the irrigation infrastructure has been developed for surface water supply covering 854,000 hectares. Of this, the farmers manage 590,000 hectares (69%) and the government 264,000 hectares (31%). The groundwater irrigation system exists only in the Terai covering 206,000 hectares, of which 84% is managed by the farmers and 16% by the government. There are 46,000 shallow and 400 deep tube wells in Nepal, but they are not used for year-round irrigation because of high operating cost.

In other words, 37% (totalling 492,000 hectares) of the Terai's irrigable land and 50% (totalling 214,000 hectares) of the mountains' irrigable land could still be brought within the irrigation system. That means Nepal could provide irrigation to an additional 700,000 hectares of cultivable land.

The irrigation need of Nepal looks so small compared to abundance of river water. The big rivers like the Koshi and the Gandaki are already irrigating four million hectares in India as against a few hundred thousand in Nepal. The Karnali, the West Seti and the Mahakali are expected to irrigate on an average two million hectares each in India. Altogether the five rivers can irrigate more than ten million hectares in India but on the Nepalese side it is only half a million hectares in the Terai. As the mountainous regions cannot be serviced by the kind of network built in the Terai, Nepal's middle and high altitude sections are always thirsty, even though the water flows right from their front yard and backyard.

A cost estimate for building an irrigation system for the remaining 700,000 hectares of land has been made. The cost per hectare will be between Rs. 180,000 and Rs. 250,000 in the case of surface water supplies and from Rs. 40,000 to Rs. 70,000 for shallow and deep tube wells. The final calculation boils down to $2 billion to bring the remaining irrigable land into the irrigation system. This is equal to two years of Nepal's annual budget. In other words, Nepal is not in a position to develop an irrigation system on its own.

Chapter Fifty-Four

The Maiden Shock

The Koshi project provided the first ever gigantic shock to the Nepalese people. It was the first big 'mutually beneficial' project Nepal embarked upon at the behest of India. It turned out to be a one-sided collaboration at the cost of poor Nepal. Apart from the unequal terms, the terminology used in this water treaty does not at all give the impression that two sovereign states had signed it. The Indian government is described as the 'Union' while the Nepalese government as the 'Government'. Arguably the impression the treaty gives is that Nepal is a part of India - as if a provincial authority was signing an agreement with the central authority.

Under the agreement, India built a big barrage at Bhimnagar on the border between Nepal and India to discipline the Koshi, one of the four major river systems of Nepal. From its sheer size, it used to play havoc with the downstream Indian state of Bihar during the monsoon season. The Koshi is often compared with the Huang Ho river of China for its capacity to wreak enormous damage to Bihar.

India had originally planned to build a multi-purpose high dam in the foothills of the Siwalik range right inside Nepal to harness the Koshi for irrigation and power and for flood control. But because of the high cost, India abandoned the idea and chose a downstream site near the Indo-Nepal border for a barrage with several sluice gates. The barrage led to the flooding of thousands of hectares of fertile Nepalese land. India opted for the downstream site also, in order to be in absolute control of the project.

The agreement provided that all constructions and properties of the project would be considered as belonging to India. The roads and the barrage bridge, a vital link between the eastern and middle parts of Nepal, constructed under this project remain under India's control. They are open to use by the Nepalese only with the permission of the local Indian authorities. But all transportation facilities of Nepal in the periphery of the project are legally open to use by the Indians for the sake of safety and maintenance of the project.

Similarly, India is entitled freely to use all the communications facilities existing in Nepal in the interests of the project. But the facilities set up by India are not open for local use. Except for matters relating to law and order, Nepal has handed over, under the treaty, all administrative powers to India. The Nepalese have also been denied fishing rights within two miles of the barrage and embankments.

Nepal made a substantial contribution to the project including material for a 20 mile long and 675 feet wide stretch of railway line, a chunk of land 10 miles long and 675 feet wide for the western embankment and a third chunk of about 80 square miles. Nepal also allocated 33 hectares of fertile land for housing and 135 hectares for other purposes. Also provided was a chunk 12 miles long and 66 feet wide and another 10 miles long and 66 feet wide for setting up the railway lines. Nepal also provided, free of cost, huge volumes of timber, stones, sand, elephants, and firewood for the labour force.

The agreement mentions the potential irrigation benefits to Nepal but keeps the nature and magnitude of similar gains to India secret. It was apparently done to avoid differences in sharing irrigation benefits. The Koshi project provided for irrigation in Nepal for about 87,000 hectares of land. Later developments established that India was using irrigation facilities from this project in about 2 million hectares, twenty-three times more than that of Nepal. It is a matter of coincidence that India is twenty-three times bigger than Nepal.

The most humiliating part of this project is that India controls all the water. The irrigation systems built on Nepal's side are solely dependent on the whims of the Indian officials in charge of the project. In the lean season when the Nepalese farmers need water, it is not made available because that affects the flow of water into the Indian systems.

The Koshi agreement provides navigation facilities to Nepal through Indian rivers. This turned out to be wishful thinking because over the last four decades or so no such facility has ever been created for use.

The Koshi barrage has saved thousands of lives and hundreds of billions worth of property in India by way of flood control. India refuses to recognise the benefit she has acquired from this project for fear that Nepal might demand a share of sorts.

At the time of signing of this agreement, the real issues were all pushed under the carpet of diplomatic niceties and the ideals of neighbourly considerations. The shock, nevertheless, has not receded.

◆

Chapter Fifty-Five

The Bottomless Pit

The Indo-Nepal Koshi project agreement of 1954 provided that India would build two Koshi-fed irrigation systems in Nepal as compensation for the submersion of thousands of hectares of agricultural land on the Nepalese side. Accordingly, in 1964, a follow-up agreement was signed by the two governments. The construction started and the main canal was completed in 1970 while the branch, secondary and the tertiary canals were completed in 1975. The canal is 53 km long and serves 12 tributary canals totalling 299 km and 36 direct minor canals totalling 216 km.

But no sooner was the project handed over to Nepal, than the systems started giving trouble because they were technically unsound. The headwork for acquisition of water for this canal was built at Chatara immediately downstream from the gorge where the Koshi swirls south to the plains. Water directed into the canal from the river with a lot of silt proved a major problem sooner than expected. No diversion structure was built to properly regulate the flow of water. The second intake which was built further down posed yet another problem. The river took a separate course, leaving the system high and dry.

The farmers in the affected area are never happy with the performance of this canal. Firstly, they did not get water when they needed it the most. During the rainy season, the supply was excessive. The excess water in the fields resulted in reduced crop yield. Siltation, on the other hand, drove sand into the field affecting its fertility. Resentment of the farming community had its impact on the local economy.

India handed over the irrigation project to Nepal in 1976 and within two years Nepal had to seek a substantial amount of credit of $30 million from the World Bank for its repair. The Nepalese government had to put in its share of $7.5 million. The total amount was meant for the rehabilitation and improvement of the irrigation and drainage systems in the command area. The works concluded in 1986.

Soon after, another investment had to be made for further improvement in the irrigation system. In 1987, the World Bank granted $49.9 million for this project, of which $40 million was in the form of a soft loan and the rest a grant. But that too was no cure for the project. A third World Bank loan worth $29.6 million was sought in 1993 to build a diversion channel at the headwork, which should have been there at the outset. This costly new headwork was meant to do nothing but correct the initial mistakes. This purpose was to curb the sediment flow into the intake canal and to prevent the river flowing away from another intake point. Despite two attempts to keep the system going the end is nowhere in sight. A new plan for improvement is already afoot, with a foreign loan of course.

◆

Chapter Fifty-Six

Delay's Victim

The Western Koshi Canal is a classic example of what an irrigation system should not be. It is one of the two by-products of the Koshi Project built by India supposedly for the benefit of Nepal. The Western Koshi Canal presents a clear case of inordinate delay and doubt that resulted in untold wastage in the annals of this $5 million project. Although the main agreement between India and Nepal was signed in 1954 paving the way for the construction of this project, a subsidiary accord had to be signed in 1966, after twelve years.

Under the agreement, about 25,000 hectares of land in Nepal was to be irrigated by water diverted from the Western Main Canal, as the project was named. Implementation of this accord took ages, or so it seemed. Troubles between the two signatory countries were created by hostile public opinion on both sides of the border. After a lapse of exactly another twelve years, a fresh agreement was arrived at in 1978, in which not only the pre-planned Western Koshi Canal but also the construction of a new pumped canal and the extension of one already existing system called the Chandra canal were included. The whole business was supposed to be completed in three years. The trouble is, it took exactly ten years to accomplish the job, at least in name.

In all, then, the Western Canal irrigation system was completed on the Nepalese side thirty-four years after the Indian commitment was formalised. Naturally, the people expected it to run smoothly and be instrumental in boosting agricultural growth, especially in the Saptari district where the system was mainly located. But it proved to be a total disappointment as far as the farmers were concerned. No less frustrated were the Nepalese officials who were charged with the responsibility to operate and maintain it.

The reasons are not hard to see. The extension of this canal system supposed to be built on the Indian side remains still incomplete. India pledged to complete it by 1988 but did not. That leaves the system technically faulty. As a result water is not released in adequate amounts, and without adequate water the Nepalese canal does not work. Moreover, as the water is mainly controlled by the Indian project officials, there is no certainty in the supply of water in the Western Canal system. Also, the Nepalese project managers have not been able to develop a rapport with the farmers in the command area.

The impact of the main canal, which is 112 km long and the pumped canal which is 41 km long is practically nil. While the fields near the main canals are swamped due to seepage from the canals, there is a lack of water towards the tail-end of all the functioning canals. Out of the thirteen channels made to take water from the main canal, the last four are useless owing to faulty design.

Water does not reach the end of the irrigation distribution system. This is borne out by the fact that in four tributaries designed to function at full supply, no water has ever entered. The low supply of water is attributed to the construction of a similar system on the Indian side of the border. As the key to the water supply lies in India's hands, the advantage goes to India. It does not matter what happens on the Nepalese side.

The story of the pump project, which is 41 km long with eleven subsidiary canals, is no less revealing. The far reaches of the system receive water only once during late summer when there is no need for water. That led the farmers to infer that the canal is a drainage, not an irrigation canal. On top of that, the indiscriminate use of pumping sets in the main canal caused heavy damage to the embankments. Often the project has to be declared closed either because of no secured water supply or no pump operator.

The lift irrigation system was also found to be too expensive as the electricity bill, even though subsidised, was awesome. Moreover, the system was entirely dependent on the fluctuating moods of the Indian officials in charge of the power station.

The net result of all these man-made dampers is that the Western Canal supplies water to only 400 hectares of land (against its target of 11,300 hectares), a mere 3.5% during the *kharif* (summer crop) season and half of it during *rabi* (winter crop) season. As far as the pump canal is concerned, it supplies water to 5,000 hectares out of the target of 13,000 hectares during *kharif*, an impressive 38% and 1,000 hectares during *rabi* season. Put together it comes to 7% of the target total. But in the drought of 1992, when pumps worked non-stop, the total energy bill jumped to Rs. 10 million. It goes without saying that the bill owed to the Nepal Electricity Authority, the sole supplier of power, remains unpaid.

◆

Chapter Fifty-Seven

Nepal's Niagara

One fine morning in 1996, the Nepalese government announced that an agreement had been signed between Nepal and India to build a high dam on the Koshi river. For those unable to understand the implications, it was just more run-of-the-mill development news. But for those in the know it was a mammoth shock. To them an insult was added to injury. Having been bled so much by the first Koshi project, how did Nepal fall for yet another trap?

The idea of erecting a high dam on the Koshi river, not only for irrigation and hydropower production but also for flood control and waterways, was first suggested some fifty years ago. The feasibility report prepared by India in 1981 proposed a 269 metre high dam which would generate 3,300 MW of electricity and irrigate 1.5 million hectares of land. A reservoir as big as 256 square km, equal to the area of two districts of Nepal, would be built to store 13,450 million cubic metres of water. The amount of water thus stored would be enough to flood the whole of the Bihar state in India. The cost was estimated at $1,170 million.

Studies on this high dam were commissioned from time to time. A JICA-funded study made on behalf of Nepal recommended a 239 metre dam to save a place called Kurule from submersion. That spot is considered appropriate for a diversion of Sunkoshi (a tributary of the Koshi river) water to an adjacent river called the Kamala. The objective of this diversion through a 16.6 km long tunnel is to generate 93 MW of electricity and irrigate 175,000 hectares of land within Nepal. The projected cost of the high dam project was $2,770 million, which was more than double the Indian estimate. The cost of the Sunkoshi diversion is a separate issue.

The Nepalese government claimed that the proposed high dam would bring about a green revolution in mid Nepal's Terai since it would facilitate diversion of water from the Sunkoshi river to the Kamala river which already had a large network of irrigation canals. But going by the sad experience with the numerous irrigation facilities in existence for the last forty years like the Narayani, the Bagmati, the Kamala, the Koshi pump canal and the Koshi Western Canal, the people could not possibly take the official claims at their face value.

The accord of 1996 contained such provisions that sounded suspicious. For instance, Nepal was asked to provide all technical data and information regarding the flow of water from the Nepalese rivers under this watershed to India on a regular basis. The Koshi has a total watershed of 92,538 square km of which 41,333 square km lies in Nepal. No provision for a reciprocal supply of relevant information was made.

The accord also provided for the establishment of Indian research centres in Biratnagar, Janakpur, Dharan, Birgunj and Kurule in Nepal to carry out hydrological and other related studies pertaining to the proposed dam. Once again the principle of reciprocity was not followed.

According to the accord, India will bear all the expenses of the feasibility study of the proposed dam. It will also pay the daily allowances of the Nepalese technicians and officials involved in the project study. This hurt the sentiments of many Nepalese who strongly believe that the accord amounts to a sell-out as far as Nepal's vital interests are concerned.

The accord is also deemed against the spirit of the Nepalese constitution which clearly stipulates that all international accords involving the water resources of Nepal require endorsement by a two-thirds majority of parliament.

There is yet another group of people in the Nepalese administration who want the height of the proposed dam increased to 350 metres so that a new waterway could be opened between Chatara of Nepal and the confluence of the Ganges in India, stretching 165 km. This, if ever enforced, would enable Nepal to directly ship its international cargo from the port of Calcutta without going through the cumbersome and costly overland route to the sea.

Although the high dam idea had been tentatively approved by India and Nepal way back in 1949 it was put on hold for want of adequate resources - Rs. 1,770 million. So as a makeshift option, the Koshi project with its barrage and embankments was built in 1954.

Environmentalists too are upset by the idea of a high dam because it is an outmoded concept. Moreover, Nepal being an earthquake prone zone, such a dam would be a sword of Damocles for the people downstream, especially in Bihar for benefit of whom this engineering folly is being contemplated. What an irony.

The dam is estimated to have a life span of one hundred years. That means it will be completely filled by slit rolling down the mountains over this period. Do we then let the Koshi cascade down from an enormous height of about 300 metres? Will this 'Niagara Falls' of Nepal be a boon for tourism or a bane for ecology?

◆

Chapter Fifty-Eight

The Second Shock

Hardly had the shock the Nepalese got from the Koshi river project diminished, than a much bigger second shock was unleashed. It came in the form of yet another water accord between Nepal and India - the Gandak agreement. Just five years after the Koshi agreement was signed, the Gandak accord was thrust upon the Nepalese on 4th December, 1959.

The so-called bilateral deal was vehemently opposed in parliament as well as the streets of Nepal. The majority administration of Nepali Congress, despite protests, went ahead with the deal and although the then prime minister B.P. Koirala had pledged that he would table the agreement document in parliament, he did not do so. Another river of Nepal was then 'sold out' to the southern neighbour.

Under this agreement, India built a barrage, half of which lay in Nepal and the other half in India. Basically an irrigation project, it required the construction of canal head regulators on the Gandak (Narayani) river at Tribeni near the Indo-Nepal border.

Under this project, a western and an eastern canal were proposed for irrigation of about 60,000 hectares of land in Nepal, 16,000 hectares in the west and 44,000 hectares in the east. The western canal was built in Nepalese territory. But for irrigating the eastern part of Nepal, India built a 94 km long Don Branch canal in Bihar (India) to supply 24 cubic metres of water per second to the Nepal border on a regular basis. In other words, Gandak river water travelled from Nepal to India and then again from India to Nepal. Both canal systems proved to be utterly unworkable, vindicating the critics' fear that all India wanted to do was exploit Nepal by offering a few lollipops.

As far as the irrigation prospects from this India-oriented project were concerned, the agreement maintained an ominous silence. However, later developments revealed that India had actually been irrigating more than 2 million hectares adjoining Nepal. It meant India was benefiting at least 33 times more than Nepal. The discrepancy will grow simply because the irrigation system on the Indian side works at optimum level whereas the one on the Nepalese side is totally dependent on water controlled by India.

The agreement guarantees a minimum flow of water to the project from the Gandak river whose watershed area spreads over a large part of mid-western Nepal. Under this agreement, Nepal has forfeited its right to use its own natural resource - water - because the said resource cannot be used in a way that might adversely affect the project. In other words, Nepal cannot divert the Gandak water to other regions or valleys for irrigation nor for other purposes as it might reduce the volume of water in the river.

Nepal has not only provided land for the project but virtually ceded it to India. Although the agreement states that Nepal's sovereign right over the land made available to the project would remain undisturbed, the statement is undercut by another provision under which India holds the right to such land as long as it pays rent to Nepal at the going rate. Nepal received some financial compensation for the land which, the agreement says, India would return if it so chooses to do in future.

A rankling provision in the Gandak accord has it that all constructions under the project are Indian properties. The bridge over the barrage is open to the Nepalese only as long as the Indian authorities allow it. The Nepalese can use the telephone and wireless facilities only if the Indian officials so desire. Even the roads built under the project on Nepalese territory cannot be used by the Nepalese without their permission.

In contrast, though, India can freely move its personnel and use communication facilities, and has unrestricted freedom to carry out hydraulic, hydrometric, hydrological and geological surveys in the area. No wonder the Gandak project stands today as a thorn bleeding the Nepalese heart.

◆

Chapter Fifty-Nine

The White Elephant

The Narayani irrigation system (also known as the West Gandak Canal) is the direct product of the Gandak project. The project comprises two systems, one to irrigate 16,000 hectares on the western side of the Nawalparasi district and the other on the eastern side to irrigate 42,000 hectares in the Narayani zone in the Nepalese Terai. For this, India built a 94 km long Don Branch canal to supply Nepalese water to Nepal, through India. The project was handed over to Nepal in 1976.

However, the design and implementation standards were so inferior that the system did not work at all. As no subsidiary canals and structures were constructed, the project could not maintain a water supply in a reliable and satisfactory fashion.

It was before the formal handing over of the project that Nepal started spending money on the system although it was India's sole responsibility to complete it.

By 1973, the Nepalese government had invested $10 million supplemented by a $6 million soft loan from the World Bank. The allocation was originally meant for improving the 62 km long eastern canal covering the command area of 28,700 hectares. But in 1977, the target was slashed to 27 km covering 16,000 hectares, apparently because of the unsatisfactory original design.

Since the first set of improvements was not enough to set the project right, further help was sought. The second effort came about in 1978 with $17 million, of which $14 million came from the World Bank. It took eight years to accomplish the 'improvements ' in the main canal systems and construct secondary canals, drains and service roads.

More help was needed to keep it going. This time around, $35.5 million was allocated, the major portion again coming from the good old World Bank. The objective was to extend the command area (8,000 hectares) under the eastern canal in the Rautahat district. But the target had to be abandoned in favour of more urgent works repairs to previous works which were devastated in the 1985 floods.

The irrigation structure India created at the cost of $20 million under the Gandak project covered about 37,500 hectares of land. But within twenty years of operation, Nepal ended up spending more than three times ($ 62.5 million) for repair and maintenance.

Was it worth the money and effort? Today, the Narayani zone irrigation system is regarded as a white elephant with no benefits for crop growth. The weakest link is the inability of the Nepalese officials to announce the exact dates when there will be a water supply in the canal. Why? The key is in the hands of Indian officials. Even the volume of water depends on the whims of Indian authorities.

The Gandak barrage has been built just over the border, the eastern part lying in India and the western part in Nepal. The eastern canal passes through the Indian territory for over 94 km over which Nepalese officials have no say whatsoever. This canal which was damaged by floods in 1988 could not supply water for five years to Nepal as India took that long to repair it. Even when it operates, it has never been able to supply more than 500 cusec against the treaty commitment of 850 cusec of water.

The problem started right in the beginning thanks to Indian goodwill towards 'friendly' neighbour Nepal. As the system was put in operation it was immediately discovered that the infrastructure built to cover 900 hectares was awfully inadequate for water distribution. The embankment was not high enough, nor were safeguards against river floods and erosion of the banks good enough. No wonder then that only half of the planned command area receives irrigation water during *kharif* season and only 20% of that area is fit for *rabi* crops.

◆

Chapter Sixty

The Dying Dam

The Sarada dam built in 1928 is the oldest monument of Nepal's misery caused by utilisation of her water resources by foreigners. The dam was born out of a 1920 agreement between Nepal and British India providing for a barrage on the Mahakali river in western Nepal. Since the river where the dam was built flowed through Nepalese territory, Nepal agreed to concede over 2,898 acres (1,173 hectares) of land to India in exchange for the same amount of land elsewhere. No trace of that promised land is visible today. In practical terms, the land given to India was some sort of a Nepalese donation to India.

The barrage lies at the southern end of Nepal's western frontier with India. The Sarada barrage was designed in such way that Nepal could use only a minuscule part of the total volume of water released from the dam. The main canal on the right bank has the capacity of discharging 396 cubic metres per second to India. The canal on the left bank serving the Nepalese side could discharge only 28 cubic metres of water per second, fourteen times less.

In addition to the discriminatory sharing arrangement between the two countries, the headwork has been constructed to Nepal's disadvantage. The headwork on the Nepalese side has been connected to the main canal by a 1.1 km long conveyance canal on Indian territory, a part of which had been donated by Nepal. In other words, the main canal is regulated by the Indians who also control how much water goes in to the conveyance canal. The visitors to the site cannot miss the difference between the Indian and Nepalese canals. While the Indian canals are always brimming with water, the Nepalese canals are either dry or at best half full.

The special feature of the project is that India used it for her unilateral benefit for about fifty years since its inception in 1928. Nepal only started building an irrigation infrastructure in 1971 at a cost of $2 million for an area of 3,200 hectares of land but it was made possible only after lush green dense forest cover was removed for human settlement.

The first attempt succeeded in creating higher quality canals on the Nepalese side but, as it usually is the case, they did not perform well. Subsequently more and more money had to be pumped into this project. At the start of the 1980s decade almost $20 million had already been spent in expanding the command area to 4,800 hectares. The World Bank lent $16 million to this project. Before the credit was extended, the UNDP had already spent $200,000 on studying the project's feasibility.

As the decade of the 1990s began, a fresh allocation of $26.3 million was made available with the World Bank providing $23.3 million. This time around, the irrigation facility was to be extended over 6,800 hectares. Thus, an incredible total of $48 million was spent by Nepal to irrigate just 14,800 hectares. The ultimate dream is to provide irrigation facilities to 23,000 hectares of land from this project.

But will it ever come true? It looks tough. The canal construction contract was last awarded to an Indian company. Due to utter slackness in work the contract has been cancelled. Equipment and project-related property belonging to the company were confiscated by the Nepalese government. Although a new contractor is being sought through an open competition, there is no way Nepal can avoid bearing the brunt of extra costs.

The other reason for doubt over the realisation of Nepal's dream is the moribund character of the 70 year old Sarada dam. It is precisely with that in mind that India built the controversial Tanakpur dam some 7 km upstream of the existing Sarada barrage in the eighties. The apparent aim may be to generate 120 MW of power, but the real one is to discard the Sarada project. India, in fact, planned to divert water from the Tanakpur dam straight into its own canals hitherto served by the Sarada dam. Had that happened the whole irrigation complex on the Nepalese side would have been left high and dry.

Responding to Nepal's protests, India agreed to revert the Tanakpur water to the Mahakali river, after using it in the generation of 120 MW, so that the Sarada barrage could still be used until it died a natural death. At the moment, the canal of the Tanakpur dam has been constructed to serve the Sarada barrage. But over a period of time, the whole network of irrigation canals on the Nepalese side could be rendered redundant as the great Sarada dam vanishes in the Himalayan thin air. Although the Mahakali Treaty has made provision to supply water to Nepal from the Tanakpur dam, equal to the volume being consumed from the Sarada dam, such an outlet at the Tanakpur dam is likely to face a technical problem in carrying out this promise.

◆

Chapter Sixty-One

The Illegitimate Baby

In the eyes of Nepal, the Tanakpur Dam was built illegally by India on the Mahakali, a border river. But India said it was being built since 1983 on her own territory.

The real reason behind this unilateral construction was the realisation that the days of the seventy-year-old Sarada Dam, about seven km downstream, were numbered. From the Indian point of view it was therefore wiser to build a dam meant for her exclusive benefit.

India subsequently planned to construct the Tanakpur Dam to supply the Mahakali river water to a powerhouse through a 566 metre long canal and then to irrigate half a million hectares of land in India. It meant total diversion of water from the joint Sarada barrage, drying up the canal on the Nepalese side.

Nepal protested against India's design to deprive Nepal of the irrigation water from the Mahakali river. India listened to the Nepalese grievance but asked for cooperation to let it build the left afflux bund on the Nepalese territory. Before the talks were concluded, Nepal was caught up in momentous political turmoil. While the Nepalese were engaged in launching the democratic movement against the direct autocratic rule of the King, India went ahead with the construction of the Tanakpur Dam on Nepalese territory without any formal permission.

That could have stood as a sore point between India and Nepal but the new democratic government headed by G.P. Koirala endorsed India's arbitrary action in 1991.

A memorandum of understanding was signed by Nepal legitimising the 577 metre long left afflux bund on the Nepalese territory. As if that wasn't enough, Nepal also allowed use of 2.9 hectares of its territory for the Tanakpur barrage. In return, India agreed to supply 7 MW of power (out of 120 MW of produced power) to Nepal free of cost, to supply 150 cusecs (4.25 cubic metre per second) of water from the Tanakpur barrage to irrigate about 2,500 hectares of Nepalese land and to connect the Tanakpur barrage with the East-West Highway of Nepal, a matter of just a few kilometres.

Before the ink was dry on this so-called 'understanding' between India and Nepal, massive opposition in parliament as well as on the streets, ensued to force the government to change its stand. Legal suits were filed against the official claim that 'understanding' did not require parliamentary ratification.

The Nepalese constitution clearly stipulates that any treaty of serious, extensive and long-term consequences on water and other natural resources of Nepal must be endorsed by a two-thirds majority of parliament.

The opposition pleaded in the Supreme Court that the accord on Tanakpur was not an 'understanding' but a 'treaty' in the first place and is, therefore, subject to parliamentary endorsement by a two-thirds majority. Since the government had no requisite strength in parliament the motion was never submitted for debate and vote.

The Tanakpur dam was an illegal structure as far as Nepal was concerned. It remained so until due approval of Nepal was obtained. But that did not make any difference to dam operation and use of water by India. Legitimacy to the project eventually came through when a bigger Mahakali Integrated Development Treaty was signed between Nepal and India in 1996.

Besides overriding previous bilateral agreements on the Sarada and Tanakpur, the new agreement, ratified by Nepal's parliament by a two-thirds majority, opened up a new horizon for the development of a mega multi-purpose project at Pancheshor, further up the Mahakali river.

The new facility that India agreed under this umbrella agreement regarding the supply of water is called the Brahmadev irrigation project. This project is not only fraught with political problems but also loaded with technical weaknesses. The pond level of the Tanakpur reservoir is located at 246.7 metres. The head regulator on the Indian side is at an elevation of 241.5 metres. India has constructed for Nepal a small head regulator on the left embankment at the level of 245 metres. It is located way upstream to impede the smooth flow of water to Nepal. Experts think that this has to be remodelled if the promised supply of water is to be had. The Brahmadev project, estimated to cost $10 million, seems to be in trouble long before it is completed.

◆

Chapter Sixty-Two

A Pandora's Box

The Mahakali River Agreement between Nepal and India is a Pandora's box overflowing with all the intricacies that one could possibly conceive of in its technical, financial, diplomatic and political terms. In fact, there is no such thing as the Mahakali project. The Mahakali is a snow-fed river that separates Nepal and India in the west before it merges with the Ganges. The river is seen as a source of power and, by implication, prosperity for the peoples of Nepal and India. With that belief, the 1996 treaty was concluded for the integrated harnessing of this river for electricity, irrigation and flood control. It is comprehensive in the sense that it embraces the legacies of the past, be it the Sarada irrigation system or the Tanakpur dam. The future remains to be seen as the Pancheshor high dam project gets under way. After all is said and done, Nepal stands to lose more than it hopes to gain.

The new agreement has endorsed inequitable distribution of water from the seventy-five year old Sarada barrage by allocating 16.25 cumecs of water to Nepal and 248 cumecs to India. India will continue to receive fifteen times more water than Nepal, as has been the case over the last seven decades.

From the Tanakpur project, Nepal will get 7 MW out of the 120 MW of power generated from it. It has also been allocated 28.35 cumecs during the rainy season and 8.50 cumecs during the dry season through a proposed canal system. India's biggest gain from this agreement is that it legitimises the Tanakpur project which, as said earlier, was illegally erected on Nepalese territory without permission. India also secured continued irrigation of half a million hectares of its land in case the ageing Sarada dam calls it a day. Under such an eventuality, Nepal's existing irrigation complex completed at a cost of $46 million might go awry despite a provision made to supply the required volume of water to it from the Tanakpur Dam.

The proposed Pancheshor project is a big enigma. The story is too tall to be credible. There is an initial proposal to erect a monumental dam of 315 metres in height with capacity of generating 6,480 MW power and irrigating 1,703,000 hectares of land. The total outlay of the project is around $3 billion at 1995 prices. However, Nepal and India have yet to finalise the detailed project report (DPR) on the Pancheshor high dam enterprise. The estimated cost and benefits may actually be nothing but a wild guess.

Nonetheless, the Nepalese government is feeding the population with a sweet dream of transforming their lives from the state of utter poverty to unprecedented affluence. According to the official version, Nepal will earn $313 million annually from the export of power to India alone. But the price at which the electricity will be sold out to India after ten years has not been ascertained. Even the modalities of the pricing pattern have not been agreed upon between the two countries. At any rate India will be the 'monopoly' buyer of Nepal's hydropower.

The belief is that since India will have the upper hand, it will agree to pay the lowest possible price. She is not obliged to buy power from Nepal while Nepal has to sell it to India. Hence, the expected millions of dollars from the sale of electricity to India may very well be a mirage.

In terms of flood control and irrigation, the official figure itself admits that 99% of the benefits would accrue to India and only a paltry 1% to Nepal. In monetary terms, India will benefit by $203.4 million whereas Nepal will get $1.5 million from extra irrigation facilities created under the project. In the domain of flood control, the benefits to India are $3 million and to Nepal only $0.7 million per annum.

But the cost-sharing ratio is not at all commensurate with benefits ratio. The official estimate of investment is $960 million for India and $246 million for Nepal (a fourfold difference), whereas the difference in benefits is ninety-three times in favour of India.

Apart from the yawning gaps between the estimated benefits to India and Nepal, the treaty is full of faults. The issues of consumptive rights of the contracting parties, water rights accruing from the border river, resource mobilisation, project implementation and so forth have been raised on both sides of the border. This means that controversies will continue to pester the project throughout. The Mahakali treaty has revealingly not ruffled any feathers in India. The reason? Because enormous benefits are going to the Indians, the types of benefits they have been aspiring to for decades since winning freedom from the then imperial Britain.

Chapter Sixty-Three

Myth and Reality

The Pancheshor project, like many other mega projects in Nepal, has created a myth. A virile public debate over the issue of whether Nepal should go for the multi-billion dollar hydroelectric project with India ensued as soon as the proposal was made public. At that point it was claimed that Nepal would benefit by Rs. 120 billion ($2 billion) a year on the completion of the project. The myth was promptly exploded as no one could believe in the wildest of dreams that a project which is estimated to cost $3 billion in total would yield $2 billion revenue annually. People in Nepal listened in awe and utter disbelief to tales about this hidden treasure of theirs. But it all disappeared in no time, as a mocking bird would, because reality is always entirely different from myth.

The Nepalese government also claimed that this project, following the Indo-Nepal Mahakali Treaty, would do miracles for the country - would open the floodgate of foreign investment, double the people's per capita income and upgrade the nation's status from a poor to a rich economy. As if that wasn't all, the project would offset the adverse balance of payments with India, which currently stands at Rs. 20 billion ($333 million). The treaty was formally signed by the government and was subsequently endorsed by the Nepalese parliament. None of those promises were forthcoming from it though. Having done the job, the myth of miracles vanished into thin air.

Nepal wants the Pancheshor project to have a 315 metre high dam to generate 6,480 MW of power by building a storage facility capable of retaining 9.72 billion cubic metres of water in the foothills of the mountains straddling both Nepal and India. The purpose is to produce as much power for as possible for export. But India has proposed a smaller dam, meaning lower power production. She is talking about a 262 metre high dam with storage of 5.15 billion cubic metres of water to produce 1,750 MW of electricity.

Whether the two countries will ever agree on the size of the dam is itself a big question. Even if they do come to an accord on the matter, the question of finding the necessary resources and mode of implementation remains, upsetting all cost-benefit calculations made so far. It thus shows that the claims of the Nepalese government are phoney and based on wishful thinking, to say the very least.

The agreement supplies yet another myth of equity in cost and benefit sharing with regard to power. According to official figures, Nepal will have to invest $848.4 million whereas India will put in $927.7 million. Annually, Nepal and India are each supposed to earn from power generation $313.4 million. Since Nepal cannot in the foreseeable future consume its share of power (thousands of MWs) it naturally has to sell it to somebody else. However, the treaty obliges Nepal to sell its excess power only to India at a mutually agreeable price. Nepal cannot sell power to a third country, say China, even if it becomes feasible at some future date. That makes Nepal's position vulnerable. In other words, India can virtually dictate the price of Nepalese power. There are no set principles stating how the price of electricity to be sold by Nepal to India should be determined. The hoped for income from power export to India is thus only an expectation which may not be fulfilled.

It is the irrigation potential that is enormous. A command area of 1,703,000 hectares can be served. Of this, 1,610,000 hectares will be irrigated in India and 93,000 hectares in Nepal. For this, India will annually use 449 cumecs of water as against Nepal's 118 cumecs.

The total benefit from irrigation is estimated at $204.9 million every year, of which $203.4 million will go to India and $1.5 million to Nepal. In terms of flood control, India will gain $3 million as against Nepal's $0.7 million. Broadly calculated, Nepal gains 1% of the total benefits accruing from irrigation and flood control whereas India gains 99%. In terms of cost, though, Nepal will bear

23% and India 77%. Yet, it is doggedly claimed to be an equal treaty between two sovereign nations.

The treaty was also widely canvassed to have granted equal rights to the contracting parties to the use of Mahakali river water. But let us see how it works out. On completion of the Pancheshor project, there will be 726 cumecs of water flowing into the Mahakali river. Out of this volume, 10 cumecs of water will be left in the natural bed to maintain its ecology. That way, there will be 716 cumecs of water which should be divided equally between the two countries. But it is not going to work out that way. From this stock of water, India will use 248.4 cumecs invoking its consumptive right, meaning that it had been using that much water in previous projects. Under the so-called consumptive right Nepal can use only 41 cumecs of water. It means India will take six times more water than Nepal on the basis of what is also called the 'the right of first use'.

The treaty says that the principle of equal sharing will also be applied to the remaining portion of water. Water in this category comes to about 426.6 cumecs. Divided by two, India and Nepal each get 213.3 cumecs. However, both countries will not be able to consume all the water by themselves and as the estimates go, India will have an excess of 12.81 cumecs and Nepal 135.78 cumecs of water. This particular portion of water, when let out of the reservoir, can still be used in India's downstream areas. India once again benefits from Nepal's share of unused water. India refuses to pay Nepal anything for this extra water. Calculated broadly, Nepal ends up using only 17% of the total water from this project as per the Mahakali treaty. The claim of equity in water is, one might say, a well-disguised hoax.

◆

Chapter Sixty-Four

Too Good to Be True

Can Nepal, whose national annual budget is worth $1 billion, afford to forfeit an income ranging from $1.75 to $2.5 billion a year? That is what Enron, an American energy company, said Nepal was precisely doing by not installing the much talked about mega hydroelectric project on the Karnali river in mid-west Nepal.

Why does not Nepal build this project, considered by far the cheapest and therefore the most attractive not only in Nepal but also in whole of Asia? The simple answer is that Nepal has neither the requisite resources ($9 billion) nor the technical and managerial know-how to handle such a gigantic project. Whether Nepal needs a project of such magnitude producing 10,800 MW of power and irrigating 3 million hectares of land is yet another million dollar question. Nepal with a population of 20 million and $200 annual per capita income can neither consume that much electricity for another century nor does it have a territory vast enough to absorb the estimated windfalls in terms of irrigation.

So the whole idea of developing the Karnali project is for the Indian market. India's northern region contiguous to Nepal is already starving for power by over 20,000 MW and the whole Gangetic belt is in need of water to irrigate land for increased agricultural production. India is constantly on the lookout for an inexpensive way to feed her rising population, which has crossed the one billion mark.

But does India want power and irrigation facilities from this project to be built well inside Nepal? India certainly wants to see it implemented and has been showing keen interest in the same for the last few decades. But the problem lies in the fact that India wants to buy electricity cheap and does not want to pay a penny for the water that would irrigate millions of hectares of its land. So, nothing concrete has transpired despite thirty-five years of prolonged talks.

Two years ago a multinational company known the world over, Enron, appeared on the scene with a big package for the development of the Karnali river project. The company asked the Nepalese government to let it develop purely as a hydro-power project for which it was willing to invest $9 billion. Power would be sold to India at an optimum price, making profit for itself as well as Nepal. Enron assured Nepal that for the first fifteen years Nepal would get $74 to $130 million per year. After that period, Nepal would get at least $680 million on account of power export. In addition to that, it was estimated that Nepal would also get $40 million for the first fifteen years and after that period $330 million from royalties from the project per year. The attractions for Nepal are just too irresistible but they appear too good to be true.

The American company has come out with data to substantiate its claim that the project is viable. Its approach is no doubt no-nonsense. It said that after fifty years in operation the proposed project would be handed over to Nepal free. But within the fifty-year period, Enron would make a profit of $52 to $108 billion depending on the price of the electricity exported to India and possibly China. By no means is it an ordinary profit when one judges it against an investment of only $9 billion investment. For the first time perhaps the Nepalese were told that power produced in Nepal could also be exported to China, besides India. Enron proposes to build a 3,600 kilometre long transmission line from Nepal to Xian in China. This would perhaps be the longest power transmission line in the world. If ever built, it could serve as an international power grid between Nepal, India and China. But whether such a project is truly feasible is beyond Nepalese comprehension. Whether it is economical in terms of engineering and maintenance thereof is yet another legitimate question. But when Americans talk about it we may have to believe because we do not have any basis to challenge them on their premises. After all, they have walked on the moon. They just might adorn the great Himalayas with high-tension wires.

The Nepalese have been enamoured of this tantalising project since the 1950s when Swiss geologist Tony Hagen pointed out, for the first time, what enormous potentiality the Karnali river held for Nepal's hydropower development. Several studies were carried out by the Japanese, the Australians, the Norwegians, the Swiss, the Americans, and the Canadians in the last fifty years but to no avail. Finally, in 1980, when no agency was forthcoming, the Nepalese government itself spent a $15 million World Bank loan preparing a feasibility report on this potentially 10,800 MW monolith.

In 1985, an American company, Harza, was to get the contract for the study. The contract was subsequently changed and given unilaterally to another agency called the Himalayan Power Consultants of the Americans and Canadians. Kickbacks were suspected to have been a factor. There are no grounds to disbelieve it. If a government can change its decision for commission for a mere study contract, how can the people place their confidence in the decision makers. What guarantee is there that the officials won't be swayed by bigger commissions so visibly associated with a mega project worth billions of dollars. Whether kickbacks or the national interest will be paramount for Nepalese decision makers in a project of this proportion is open to individual guesses.

The most mysterious aspect of the Enron proposal is that it has not taken into account the irrigation prospects stemming from it. Waters regulated by this project can irrigate 3.2 million hectares in India and only 190,000 hectares in Nepal. No mention has been made regarding the use of this important by-product.

According to a Nepalese official, the irrigation benefits from the project are double that of the hydropower. He claims that the downstream benefits in terms of irrigation will be between $3,169 million and $6,338 million a year.

It is obvious then that India will be the main beneficiary. Whether the whole idea of launching the project militates against Nepal's larger interests thus becomes a logical question. The greatest fear the Nepalese have is created by the hurry with which the American company and Nepalese decision makers are trying to push the project through. India is keeping quiet because it has everything to gain and nothing to lose, Karnali or no Karnali.

◆

Chapter Sixty-Five

An Attrition Test

The Western Seti Hydropower Project has been conceived purely as a power plant generating 750 megawatt (MW) of electricity. Ninety per cent of power is meant for export to India. The cost of construction of the project is estimated to be $1 billion.

The Nepalese government has already signed two memoranda of understanding with the Snowy Mountain Engineering Corporation (SMEC) of Australia for the development of this project. Since the financial component of the project is yet to be decided upon it is not possible to ascertain the amount of benefits stemming from the plant.

However, due to the way the terms of the reference are changing, doubts have been expressed whether Nepal indeed stands to gain. The public doubts are based on:

1 . The first understanding specifically said that the Australian company would be given the licence to operate the project for thirty years and after that period it will be handed over to Nepal free of charge. But the second understanding is silent on the handing-over of the project to Nepal. After thirty years of operation, with the Australian Company the contract can be extended on the basis of financial analysis.

2. The memorandum provides that the SMEC will first realise its investment of $1 billion, meaning that Nepal will have to wait for benefits coming to it until such time that every penny of the Australian investment is recovered. In the event the project falls to make enough money to pay back the investment made on it Nepal will just have to forget about any benefits coming its way.

3. In the beginning the SMEC had agreed to supply 10% of power produced in project to Nepal free of cost. But that has been amended and now the proposal is that it will pay for that amount of power in cash. This way too, Nepal will have to wait until the whole of the investment made is recovered by the company.

4. A French study indicates that the benefits accruing from hydropower generation in this part of Nepal is three times the amount of investment. In terms of power Nepal's share in this project is restricted to only 10% of the total investment. Why? The discrepancy has never been explained.

5. Nepal's upstream fertile land in the neighbourhood of 40,000 ropanies (2,034 hectares) will be inundated by the dam water. How it will be compensated has not been spelled out. On top of that, about 4,000 people would be displaced and no mention has been made anywhere of just how they would be rehoused. Going by the earlier experience of Kulekhani hydroelectric project, one tends to believe the problem of rehousing the displaced persons would be treated with no sense of seriousness.

    Moreover, the people in the upstream region will be use of water for irrigation or drinking purposes if project proponents feel that the practice is disturbing the flow of water to the project. The villagers will have to get the permission from the Australians whenever they want water, or pay the price fixed by the company.

6. The downstream benefits by way of flood control and irrigation through the regulated flow of water from the project has been estimated at Rs. 20 billion. This benefit will go directly to India. But India will not pay in return a single penny because no agreement has been reached with respect to the downstream benefits.

7. According to another study, the input-output ratio in hydropower terms is 1:2 but in irrigation terms it is 1:4. The project has thus ignored the potential benefit from irrigation to the detriment of Nepal's larger interests.

◆

Chapter Sixty-Six

A Sugar-Coated Pill

Arun III has reigned in the firmament of hydropower development of Nepal for ten years since 1987. Many a time it was on the brink of take-off. It never did. One fine morning on 3rd August 1995, the World Bank President, Mr David Alfonsen, phoned the then prime minister of Nepal to say that the project was off as far as the World Bank was concerned. Without World Bank support, the project could not move ahead because all the donor countries had conditioned their assistance on the World Bank's involvement in the project. Thus the 'ideal' enterprise died before it was actually born.

Later developments, however, revealed that the claim that Arun III was a logical project for Nepal was flawed and meant basically to deceive the public. All through the promotion phase of the 201 MW Arun III, a sustained campaign was whipped up in Nepal and elsewhere in the world that it was the best possible option for Nepal in terms of cost, environmental safety and economic returns, but the myth exploded when confidential information stacked in the vaults of the World Bank and in Singha Durbar, the seat of power in Kathmandu, was brought to light.

The total cost of the project was estimated at $760 million. That would mean $3,500 per kW of power production, the highest at least in South Asia. The smaller projects' cost of production in Nepal and in neighbouring countries comes to $1,000 to $1,500. That makes the consumer price very high, increasing the kickback benefits going to people involved in the project.

Arun III smacked of being foul from the very beginning. The government claimed that the electricity produced from it was meant for export to India which was prepared to pay any price. It turned out this was a lie. The government later admitted that the power was for domestic consumption.

When environmentalists raised doubts over the desirability of the proposed dam under this project, the government said there would be no concrete dam. But later on, it was revealed that a dam 68 metres high was to be built to divert water through the tunnel to the powerhouse.

It was similarly claimed that there would be absolutely no environmental damage from the construction of this project. A famous Nepalese non-governmental organisation was assigned to conduct the EIA (environmental impact assessment) study. The findings were kept a well-guarded secret but when they were disclosed it was discovered that $10 million would be required to mitigate the likely environmental damage to the project area. The project had not made any provision for it.

The project also made an untenable claim that it would be located at the safest of sites. But a major earthquake hit the area a few years later. Besides, potential threats from eighty upstream glacier lakes cannot be ignored.

A 135 kilometre long approach road to the project site was initially planned over the surrounding mountain ridges. When the survey was done the road's length expanded to 192 km. The cost went up by many times. The World Bank allocated Rs. 860 million for the original estimates, but when the estimates went up, additional funding was refused. Instead, a valley road was accepted as it meant lesser length and lesser cost. The planners who wanted to build the approach road over the ridges had a populist overtone. So when the people learnt that the mountain road had been abandoned, they rose in revolt. They demanded the road, not the project.

The government argued that the project had to go ahead as the financial support of donor agencies had already been committed. Commitments made included, amongst others, the World Bank's $175 million, the Asian Development Bank's $150 million, Sweden's $30 million, Germany's DM 235 million. The impression being given was that since the whole business was a free gift, the cost was of no consequence. But the fact was that, except for a fragment, it was a package of loans.

The World Bank had laid too stringent conditions on Nepal. Nepal, for example, would not be allowed to build any projects above 5 MW capacity until the investment in Arun III was fully recovered. Nepal must raise the electricity tariff to cover loan repayment instalments. To cut a long story short, the stark reality was that Arun III was one of the most expensive projects, contrary to the official claim that it was the most feasible from the financial standpoint.

Among the donors, the Germans were believed to be looking for a suitable river site to use some spare Siemens turbines, and they found it in Arun. The Japanese who were equally eager to come to this project's aid were in fact interested in supplying electrical and other equipment. The World Bank and the Asian Development Bank had their own agenda of giving loans to earn interest. Finland was interested in installing of all things a diesel plant to supply thermal power to a hydroelectric project. The Nepalese promoters' primary motivation was the inevitable 10% or more commission.

◆

Chapter Sixty-Seven

Rise High

Kali Gandaki A is a hydro project which has been acclaimed the best and the most suitable for Nepal. The 144 MW project which is currently under construction is located in mid-west Nepal. Taking advantage of a mountain bend and natural gradient, a relatively short tunnel will suffice to divert water to a powerhouse on the other side of the mountain.

At a time when Arun III was being hotly debated, Kali Gandaki A was cited as the best alternative to the controversial Arun III in the eastern hills. Those who were opposing the Arun III on grounds of higher cost, environmental damage and strings attached to it by donor agencies were in fact advocating Kali Gandaki A as being a manageable medium-sized venture.

Despite its viability, Kali Gandaki A too was not entirely free of criticism. The criticism related to the dubious way its cost was inflated. As soon as it was decided to implement it, the cost escalated. The initial estimate was $280 million. It was hiked to $345 million when the issue was being seriously considered. In no time, the estimates climbed to $385 million, finally stabilising at $452 million.

When the global tenders were called for all the equipment and construction works, the prices quoted totalled $360 million only. In other words, the project could save $92 million from its final estimates. However it is doubtful if this amount will actually be saved, since some way will be found to spend this inflated amount on some imagined items for personal profit.

Under this project, a contract has been given to build a 28 kilometre access road from the highway to the project site. Rs. 108

million (about $1.8 million) has been allocated. The lowest bidder quoted his price Rs. 107 million (about $1.7 million), one million rupees less than the estimated cost. It was good the project would save that much. But when the contract was signed, the amount was hiked to Rs. 127 million (about $2.1 million). That means, the contract granted Rs. 20 million in excess of what the bidder had asked for. In fact, the 'excess' would land in private purses. Moreover, the project would have to bear Rs. 19 million more than originally estimated.

Similarly, in the case of the civil works, the estimated cost was $197 million. In the global bidding, the Impregilo SpA of Milan, an Italian company, came out on top for quoting the lowest price - $123 million, which is $74 million less than what the project had officially estimated. The contract was to be signed on 1st November, 1996, but the signing was postponed for more than a month with some ulterior motive. It became clear only when the same contract was signed for $133 million on 16th December, 1996. The bidder was happy with $123 million but the government gave him $10 million more. How this excess will be appropriated is not so difficult to guess.

As the works proceeded further, the project attracted additional criticisms. One of them related to alleged inconsistency in granting contracts for the construction of two transmission lines and a sub-station in Pokhara.

K&S Enterprises, the local agents of Spain's Isolux, was edged out by TATA-Marubeni. The Nepal Electricity Authority allegedly overvalued the tender of Isolux which had actually quoted the lowest price. Several lapses in its competitor's tender were detected such as no joint-venture documents and certificates of foreign experience. It is also alleged that Isolux's competitor, TATA-Marubeni, did not indicate custom duties and taxes in the price despite mandatory requirements. When the matter came out in public, the Nepalese authorities would not explain the reason why the decision went in favour of Tata-Marubeni. That obviously smacks of some foul play.

◆

Chapter Sixty-Eight

A Dead Canal

Chitwan valley, slightly south-east of Kathmandu, was once a thick hardwood forest. The Americans made it habitable by eradicating malaria in the 1950s. The last vestige of lush old greenery is the Chitwan National Park, a favourite tourist spot famous the world over for one-horned rhinos and Bengal tigers. As a newly opened valley, Chitwan is considered fertile and those who migrated there from the mountains prospered in no time. To keep the fertility and consequent prosperity intact irrigation facilities were introduced.

But thanks to foreign technical and financial inputs, Chitwan got perhaps the worst conceivable irrigation system which stands today as a glaring example of what an irrigation system should not be. This is the story of the Narayani lift irrigation project.

Already there were a number of irrigation systems operated by gravity, meaning that water was supplied from the higher to the lower plane. The Asian Development Bank (ADB) consultants did not find the conventional system feasible as a sustainable method. Instead they went for a lift irrigation system to cover the greater part of the Chitwan valley. Accordingly, they planned pumping water from the Narayani river to keep the network of canals going.

With this belief in mind, the ADB carried out a study in 1972. Small wonder, a loan of $8 million was instantly approved for the project. An unhesitant Nepalese government provided $4.5 million. The project was supposed to be completed by 1979 but it was only after a decade, i.e. in 1989, that the project was declared accomplished at an added cost of $12.5 million. The total came to exactly the double of what was originally estimated.

Meanwhile, a network of main and tributary canals were built. One main canal is about 18 km long, another 10 km long with a 23 km additional distribution system. The whole scheme was supposed to provide year-round water to 8,600 hectares of land with the help of two-stage pumping stations. The water had to be lifted 18 metres and 20 metres respectively in order to maintain the flow in the canals and distribution systems. To run the system at full capacity, supplying about 14 cumecs of water in a day, required 5 MW of power.

This lift irrigation system which was declared operational in 1989 went out of operation after three years. During the short time it was in operation, it indeed supplied water to the crop fields when there is normally plenty of rain in Nepal. The energy bill skyrocketed beyond the farmers' reach. The cost of irrigation water per hectare for one crop averaged at Rs. 3,000 which, needless to say, was not affordable. The pump sets functioned during the wet season when sediment content is pretty high in the river. That spoiled the pumps and other components of the machinery so badly that the repair cost alone came to more than Rs. 30 million (equivalent to $1 million at that time). The much-vaunted system thus died a near natural death.

◆

Chapter Sixty-Nine

Waste All The Way

To contemplate a lift irrigation system in a country with the best natural gradient is nothing less than rank stupidity. After having demonstrated proven stupidity at the Narayani lift irrigation system, which is now dead, will it not be ridiculous to go for yet another such scheme? That is precisely what was done in the Marchawar irrigation system. The Marchawar is a very fertile geographic region in Rupendehi district in western Nepal. The irrigation exercises in this part of Nepal had gone to waste, are going to waste and, in all probability, will go to waste.

The best illustration of wastage occurred in the 1960s when India built what was known as the Tinao irrigation scheme, a gift to Nepal. About Indian Rs. 15 million was invested for a canal system to irrigate about 14,000 hectares of land. A 250 metre long weir, the biggest hitherto in Nepal was also constructed for this purpose. All went to waste as soon as the Tinao river changed course right at the headwork site.

An attempt to salvage the system was made by the Nepalese government by rebuilding a new headwork in the river in the 1970s, only to be later abandoned on technical and other grounds. An alternative means to supply water to this canal system from the Gandak western canal was mooted. Although it was considered technically feasible, it was not economically viable. So, that too was forestalled. There was yet another attempt to find water for this canal system from groundwater sources. But this was not enough and thus the whole of the Marchawar area was made dependent on rain again.

Canals have remained dry for two decades. The government finally took up what came to be known as the Marchawar lift irrigation project in 1980. In ten years a pumping station at the confluence of the Dano and Tinao rivers was built, along with the main and distribution canals, at a total cost of $4.5 million -- $2.9 million from the UNCDF and $127,000 from UNDP. A further commitment of $6.4 million was made in the early 1990s by some international agencies.

It appears like a really big push to get water for the Marchawar irrigation system, come what may. The current objective is to cover 5,600 hectares of the command area through this extraordinary thirty-five year old method. Under this scheme, there is one station with sets of pumps - one set with four pumps and another with six pumps lifting water and feeding the 12 km long main canals and 150 km long distribution canals. The pumps are operated by 55 kW electric generators. At the current rate, it costs Rs. 0.42 to lift one cumec of water. So the operation of the pumps is limited to only 700 hours per year. After all these years of effort, the achievement is limited to only 2,000 hectares coverage, i.e. 35% of the target.

Thus far the irrigation system, even at reduced capacity, has been made possible by the constant presence of numerous foreign and local consultants who are in overall charge of the project. However, once they depart as the money dries up, the project is bound to go down the drain. The power cost to keep it going will be just too high for the farmers. The additional responsibility of maintaining the pumping sets and other equipment will get messier for the local villagers to handle although they are being dragged into managing the project. Strong doubts on the farmers' part regarding the economic viability of the project obviously persist.

◆

Chapter Seventy

Where Reason Fails

Babai is the name given to a medium-sized river but it has raise'
giant-sized eyebrows in the corridors of many an internation:
lending agency. They have found irrigation schemes based on th
river's water very attractive for investment. But as India resentec
what she called their unwarranted intrusion, the advance step
were retracted. The logical question is why India should object to .
project that is being built in the territory of sovereign Nepal.

The simple fact is that the downstream water is already bein
profitably used by India. Although India enjoys no right over th
water of Babai under any bilateral, trilateral or multilatera
arrangements, she felt her interests would be considerabl
compromised in the process. If India has a case at all, Nepal i
obliged to let at least 10% of the water flow down to India as pe
the international water conventions.

In fact, for over a century the Nepalese farmers in the distric
of Bardia have been using the Babai water for irrigation on abou
9,000 hectares of land through five intakes with the total capacity o.
releasing fifteen cumecs of water. The Nepalese government,
impressed as it was by the way the farmers had the initiative to
help themselves, thought of expanding the scheme in 1964.

International development agencies which were no less
impressed by what the Nepalese government was trying to do for
the local farmers in Bardia, chipped in in 1975 in order to help
realise the full potentiality of the so-called Babai irrigation project.
The international interest continued with UNDP extending
co-operation in the formulation of a concrete plan. Then came the

World Bank with a package containing technical as well as financial back-up.

International help for this project came mainly because they found it technically and economically viable. According to a tentative plan, it was decided to expand the Babai command area to 40,000 hectares. The survey carried out in this connection at a cost of $600,000 discovered that about one third of the command area (13,500 hectares) could be irrigated with water directly fed by the Babai river. Two-thirds of the command area (26,500 hectares) could be covered by diverting water from a neighbouring river called Bheri to the Babai river.

The proposal was to divert only 35 cumecs of water from the Bheri river which is bigger. The additional benefit of Bheri to Babai diversion was the possibility of generating 100 MW of power, thanks to the difference in elevation between Bheri and Babai. No tunnelling was required. Exactly the same had been done by India in the controversial Tanakpur project.

It was smooth sailing till 1982. By that time, the World Bank had granted $3.5 million credit to complete a detailed engineering study. But suddenly, India twisted the arms of the World Bank to force their exit from this project on the untenable ground that no bilateral agreement existed between upstream Nepal and downstream India on sharing water from these two rivers.

In fact, there was no need for any agreement between Nepal and India on the matter. But reason has its own limits. It did not prevail in this particular case. The international lending agencies were just not quite ready to earn the ire of a big country like India although they were fully aware of India's unreasonableness. The agencies tried to have the matter cleared with the Indian government but no positive response was forthcoming. So they discreetly sneaked out of the deal.

However, Nepal did not relent and pursued for funds in the international market. The Kuwaiti Fund agreed to help Nepal. Negotiations were completed and as the final agreement was scheduled for signing in early 1994, suddenly Kuwait cancelled the loan programme, again under Indian pressure.

Since the Nepalese government was already committed to develop this project it decided to go ahead with it regardless. India did not say anything thenceforth because it had no legal propriety to object to the use of water from these rivers by Nepal within her own territory.

The Nepalese government spent about Rs. 800 million until 1993 constructing the Babai headwork, a 270 metre long weir-cum-bridge and a desilting basin. But the money was not enough to complete the whole project primarily based on diversion of water from Bheri to Babai. So the project, though very profitable from Nepal's point of view, is languishing for want of resources. Obviously India's logic, however unjust, prevails over Nepal's.

◆

Chapter Seventy-One

Win-Win, Lose-Lose

India basks in the glow of a win-win situation vis-a-vis Nepal in terms of water resources. It has invariably gained, is gaining and will continue to gain from bilateral as well as unilateral deals so far as the Nepalese water is concerned. The Koshi, the Gandak and the Mahakali treaties have, in the first place, assured immense benefits to India. The second category relates to irrigation networks India has developed in its territory, which are served by water from the Kankai, Babai, Bagmati, Kamala and Karnali rivers of Nepal. Thirdly, all the mega projects like the Karnali and West Seti, if undertaken under the proposed circumstances, would yield India enormous benefits from the regulated water without paying any price to Nepal in return.

When India acts with Nepal on water issues, it benefits; when it maintains silence, still it gains; when it wages a shadow war, it again wins. A big country like India would not fight an open war with a tiny country like Nepal because of likely international repercussions. In any case, India is favourably poised to hold an upper hand in all circumstances over Nepal although the latter happens to be the upstream party. In an open debate, India is always better equipped with technical data and articulate manpower against which Nepal has generally failed to take a firm and solid stand. India has been legally permitted to carry out hydrological and climatological studies in Nepalese territory. The statistics thus obtained are later used against Nepal itself. The Nepalese who are knowledgeable and competent to take a strong stand are either bought by India, marginalised by their own government or demoralised by their rent-seeking political leadership.

Despite its lose-lose position, Nepal has fought quite a few shadow battles with India in the process of developing irrigation systems in small and medium-sized rivers like the Kankai, Bagmati, Kamala and Babai. These are the rivers where Nepal made some serious efforts to develop irrigation facilities but they are also the rivers whose downstream water India has already been extensively using for irrigation. The systems are found to be both technically and economically sound but Nepal cannot accomplish them through its own resources. Hence there have been bilateral as well as multilateral negotiation for funds. Having completed the necessary studies and project designing, as the time for clinching the deal arrives, India usually goes overtime to sabotage the projects because she fears the systems downstream will be adversely affected. Nepal does not raise the issues because she believes - and rightly so - that the projects in question are well within her jurisdiction. Neither does India raise the issue in the open because she does not want to be seen as undoing Nepal's efforts to help the farming community.

The shadow boxing takes place in the corridors of the Asian Development Bank, the World Bank, the Kuwaiti Fund and the Saudi Development Fund. But to what results? For well-known reasons India wins and has won to the cost of Nepal. The World Bank and the Kuwaiti Fund backed out of the Babai, the Bagmati and the Sikta projects at the last minute. The Asian Development Bank gave in to India's pressures in the Kankai and Kamala projects. The net result is that none of these projects has been able to gain momentum on the Nepalese side, although they were launched some twenty years ago. They are moving at a snail's pace with Nepal's own resources.

The Kankai river in the eastern part of Nepal is yet another victim of India's arm-twisting tactics. Nepal conceived this multi-purpose project in 1966 to produce about 60 MW power and irrigate 67,000 hectares of land within Nepal. After a lapse of more than thirty years, no electricity has been produced and only 5,000 hectares is being irrigated, thanks to India's interventions - covert or overt.

The Kankai was considered one of the most promising projects in terms of size, economic yield and implementation strategy. The feasibility and detailed studies were instituted with ADB assistance. The ADB provided a grant of $215,000 in 1970 to prepare the detailed feasibility report. Once the report was completed, the work on the project started in 1973 to service vastly reduced coverage of only 5,000 hectares. But there was a long delay of about eight years before the project was completed with a cost overrun of $8.90 million, the major part being borne by the ADB itself

Within two years of completion of the first phase under which irrigation was provided to limited areas, the diversion weir developed some technical snag that led to another ADB loan of $4.2 million. The original cost of the headwork structure was about $1.2 million but the remedial works on the diversion structure cost an additional $4.2 million. The second phase of the Kankai project was however carried out to cover an additional command area of 2,700 hectares of land at a cost of $4.6 million, again a credit from the ADB. Thus altogether the project has cost nearly $19 million to irrigate just 5,000 hectares as against the original objective of 67,000 hectares which is a mere 7% of the target.

The project has ground to a halt at this point for want of resources. The ADB, despite being involved in it for over thirty years, has turned its back on Nepal's plea for the further assistance required to bring the project to an optimum level of irrigation and power generation. As India fears its interests would be hurt by the use of water by Nepal upstream, it has made a strong representation to the ADB not to take any further interest in the Kankai. The shadow fight has apparently gone in favour of India even as Nepal stands today as a helpless spectator of its neighbour's pressure tactics which it is too powerless to fight.

◆

Chapter Seventy-Two

Nepal's Aid to India

There was a time when India was the only giver of aid to Nepal. That was the time when India had only recently gained freedom from the British rule while Nepal had just about broken the shackles forced by the retrograde family rule (1950). India built the first ever modern road and an airport which served to open up the closed valley of Kathmandu.

Since then the Indian aid to Nepal has continued. In the 1950s and a part of 1960s India topped the list of donors. But in the decades that followed, its relative position as a donor nose-dived with the entry of more resourceful donors - Americans, Japanese, Russians, Chinese and Germans, to name the important ones.

For more than four decades, India helped Nepal in developing roads, airports, irrigation, power, agriculture, education, health, industry, posts and telecommunications, etc. under more than 120 bilateral agreements on economic and technical co-operation. India's involvement in practically all efforts to modernisation was a fact of life in Nepal.

According to official statistics, the Indian aid to Nepal totalled Rs. 4.2 billions in thirty years between 1960 and 1990. The amount would go up further if one were to take into account the aid given before and after that period.

Roughly, Nepal received Indian aid in the neighbourhood of Rs. 5 billion in the latter half of the twentieth century.

While the Indian aid to Nepal has been visible, tangible and systematically chronicled, co-operation of Nepal with India has not been adequately taken cognisance of. Over the same half a century, Nepal has performed for the enormous benefit of India.

Under the bilateral agreements between the two immediate neighbours, India is already irrigating 2 million hectares from the Koshi project, 2 million hectares from the Gandak project, and half a million hectares from the Sarada project. In addition, India is using water from the Kankai and Babai rivers to moisturise another half a million hectares of land. Thus India is using Nepalese water for almost 5 million hectares of agricultural production.

Prospects are there for irrigating an additional 5 million hectares in India from the proposed multi-dimensional Karnali, Mahakali and West Seti river projects. Thus, broadly speaking, India is poised to gain irrigation benefits in more than 10 million hectares of its land in the foreseeable future. Since there has been no price tag as such for the downstream benefits, India does not and has not paid a single penny to Nepal in return for the direct gains made so far. If the agreements remain unaltered, India will continue to reap enormous benefits from the upcoming projects without paying anything to Nepal.

To have a credible calculation of what benefits India is deriving from Nepal, one only needs to examine the difference in the crop yields from land with and without irrigation. On the Nepalese side of the contiguous border, the paddy production with improved seeds but without irrigation in one hectare comes to 2.8 tonnes. With irrigation, the production goes up to 4.5 tonnes. At the rate of Rs. 8,000 per tonne, an increase by 1.7 tonnes means an extra Rs. 13,600 per hectare.

Similarly, wheat production goes up from 1.5 tonnes to 2.2 tonnes, an increase of 0.7 tonne. At the rate of Rs. 7,000 per tonne, an additional gain of Rs. 4,900 per hectare is made by an irrigation facility.

Production of mustard per hectare goes up from 0.45 tonnes to 0.60 tonnes with irrigation. The increase of 0.15 tonnes per hectare brings an extra Rs. 3,750 at the rate of Rs. 25,000 per tonne of mustard.

In one year, the farmers can often harvest three crops of paddy, wheat and mustard. Other crops can also be had simultaneously. These have not been taken into account. Thus, the annual benefit from irrigation facility can be approximated at Rs. 22,250 per hectare of agricultural land.

Compared to Nepal, production on Indian farms covered by irrigation projects fed by Nepalese rivers is lot higher. Although agricultural yield in India compared to Nepal varies from 10% to 50% more, taking the minimum conservative figure of only 10%, the annual benefit accruing from the irrigation facility to the Indian farmer is approximated at Rs. 24,475 per hectare.

When we take the existing irrigated land acreage of 5 million hectares in India from the regulated water from Nepal for a period of thirty years, the benefits can be as high as Rs. 3,671,250 million. There are other benefits to India from the joint ventures with Nepal in terms of flood control and averted damage to life and property in India.

In total, if we compare the amount of aid India has provided to Nepal and the gains she has made from the joint projects, the difference looks staggering. Indian aid to Nepal totals Rs. 5 billion whereas the benefits it has derived from Nepalese co-operation comes to Rs. 3,671.25 billion. In that sense, India has gained a cool Rs. 3,666.25 billion more than what it has given to Nepal. That means, for every visible rupee India has donated to Nepal in the form of aid, it has gained Rs. 733.25 in return in invisible ways from Nepal. If it is not Nepal's aid to India, then what is it?

◆

Chapter Seventy-Three

Technical Follies

The modernisation spree in Nepal has an uncanny tendency to adopt new technology with derision for traditional technologies. It is in the field of irrigation that this feature has truly been noticeable. There is no problem if new technology works to the advantage of the farmers and the country. But it should be noted with profound sadness that new technology has landed the farmers in trouble and left the country with great losses. The irony is that strides taken with the help of new knowledge and technology to upgrade irrigation facilities in Nepal have exacerbated rather than alleviated poverty. It becomes all the more rankling when big projects, launched amidst great fanfare, prove injurious to the national economy.

A scrutiny of the technical standard of large and small irrigation projects has revealed that large projects are often technically flawed whereas smaller ones tend to be technically sound. Farmer-managed irrigation systems, for example, have performed much better than those managed by the bureaucrats and foreign experts.

As a proof of the pudding, the Chandra Nahar, Kankai, Kamala and the Khageri irrigation projects, all falling into the smaller category, have a proven technical standard as vindicated by the successful functioning of their intake and canal structures. In contrast, none of the large ones is in good condition. The worst technical problems were detected in the India-made Sunsari-Morang intake work. Next to it, the Bagmati barrage, Narayani lift system and Tinao headwork stand as embodiments of technically unsound enterprises.

The technical mistakes committed in the beginning have resulted in many types of operational snags. For example, extreme silt deposition has been sighted in the Sunsari-Morang and Narayani lift irrigation systems. Some of the projects - the Narayani, Kamala and Banganga - are suffering from water shortages. Some of them are saddled with non-functioning structures or short-lived structures as in the case with the Narayani, Mohana, Khutia and Chitwan irrigation projects.

With such a defective infrastructure, it is only natural that water would not be available to the farmers in the required quantities. Water at the tertiary level of the canal system is barely or not at all available. The same applies to the so-called newly created or renovated command area under the Sunsari-Morang, Banganga and Narayani projects. Quite apart from this, umpteen numbers of problems have been triggered by the presence of too many control gates demanding efficient management, which sadly, is not there.

There is a vicious circle developing in the domain of such defective projects. When the water supply becomes undependable, the farmers couldn't care less about project maintenance. The frustrated group of farmers is actually found to have vandalised the canal system to draw water. Moreover, there is no motivation for them to join the user's groups for the management of the system. So the utility of the irrigation facilities is diminished, as are the economic returns. But the liabilities generated by these schemes are too high as most of them carry huge foreign debts.

◆

Chapter Seventy-Four

Irrecoverable Cost

Nepal is an agricultural country. Nothing is surprising when the government gives special attention to the development of agriculture. Like anywhere else, irrigation plays a key role in boosting agricultural output in Nepal. The priority given to and resources expended in developing irrigation facilities is not misplaced. But the cost is touching an unprecedented high. If the costs were inevitable there would be no room for complaint. But when the costs are raised due to technical faults, planning oversights, mismanagement and other human weaknesses, it is a different story altogether. When investment pumped into creating critical facilities like irrigation goes wrong, the nation will most likely walk into a trap. That is where Nepal is heading or is. It cannot retract its commitment, nor can it extricate itself from the trap.

It has been observed that Nepal has spent about half a billion dollars over a period of thirty years, between 1965-1995, in nine big irrigation projects. The money was intended for a sustained supply of water to increase production in over 300,000 hectares of land. Since the target went radically astray, it had a telling impact on the cost recovery position. In fact, even if everything had gone as well as envisaged in the plans, there was no way all the resources borrowed from international agencies for investment in this sector would be recovered.

Besides the capital expenditure in the development of the big irrigation schemes, the government ends up bearing about 98% of the project operation and maintenance costs. The water revenue collection has been estimated at only 2% of the operational cost.

The issue being a simple one is not difficult to understand. An authentic study has established that not a single big irrigation project in Nepal has ever served the target beneficiaries in full. The supply of water is neither timely nor of sufficient volume. The government does not have the moral strength to levy a standard water charge on the users. The rate of water revenue has therefore intentionally been kept very low. Although the average operational cost per hectare of land has been estimated at Rs. 700 per year, the water charge has been fixed at Rs. 60 to Rs. 100 depending upon the level of availability. Since it is too low the officials are not enthusiastic about collecting the tax.

The story of the lift irrigation system is even worse. The project management is not in a position to pay the electricity bills, even at a subsidised rate. Between 1985 to 1992, the bills were discounted by 50% with the government compensating the rest in power supplies to the project.

In contrast to the efficiency demonstrated by the small-scale farmer-managed irrigation systems, the government-managed big irrigation systems have incurred huge expenditure, due mainly to the imposition of expensive and unsuitable technologies at the behest of expatriate consultants and donor agencies. The operational cost is too high primarily for this reason and a host of other local reasons - mismanagement; lack of participation of the beneficiaries and so on.

◆

Chapter Seventy-Five

Real or Imagined?

It is a common practice for bureaucrats to conceal data to justify their work and official position. Equally it is the duty of the researchers and analysts to verify the accuracy of whatever trickles down to the public through the official claims; and only independent assessment can get nearer the truth. In Nepal the problem is all the more pronounced. Information is withheld to camouflage inefficiency and incompetence. So, it is in this hazy context that one has to locate what is real and what is hogwash.

The total irrigated area in Nepal is officially claimed to be over a million hectares. Presumably it is more imagined than real. Many independent studies say that the actual command area coverage is less than 30% of the total target.

The study's claim is substantiated by the discrepancies in the reported and actual size of the irrigated command area of seventeen projects based in the Terai. The total command area of big and medium-sized projects is reported to be 215,620 hectares whereas the actual average annual irrigation covers only 63,000, less than 30%.

According to other statistics, nine big irrigation projects serve only 44% of the combined command area during the monsoon season and 17% during the dry season. The total claimed command area is 34,000 hectares but the actual irrigated land is 15,000 hectares during the rains and 6,000 hectares during the dry months. There is no doubt that the reported command area under the so-called large-scale irrigation systems is exaggerated for the most part.

Similar discrepancies are noticeable even in shallow tube well systems under implementation through the initiative of the Agriculture Development Bank. Available data point out there are 46,000 shallow tube wells each irrigating 4 hectares of land. The bank claims that annually 3,000 to 4,000 new wells are being dug.

Be that as it may, an independent study has found that the claim of 4 hectares coverage by one tube well is a gross overstatement. Firstly, not all the tube wells are functioning. Secondly, the bank has no mechanism to make a correct evaluation. In fact, assessment studies in several field sites have shown that only half of what the bank estimates, i.e. two hectares, is being irrigated by the functional ones.

Another example drawn from a hilly region goes on to prove that the reported size of the irrigated area is misleading, to say the least. In a place called Hyangja near Pokhara, a popular tourist destination, the project management claimed a net command area of 285 hectares, whereas a household survey indicated it to be 227 hectares. The roster pertaining to water tax showed payers put the figure at 157 hectares. Discussions with key informants have revealed that it is actually only 100 hectares.

A study of the actual command area undertaken with the help of what is called the Geographic Information System in two districts of Nepal indicated the gap between the reported and the real coverage was indeed very wide. In the district of Jhapa where the Kankai project is located the actual coverage was found to be around 46% of the reported area. In Chitwan district, the irrigation coverage made by the Khageri scheme was found to be 42% of the claimed command area. The Panchakanya project covers only 38%.

◆

Chapter Seventy-Six

The Untimely Delivery

Before the modern development bug penetrated Nepal, the Nepalese banked on their traditional wisdom and knowledge to help themselves in every aspect of life. When the development wave swept Nepalese society, the old tended to make way for the new. The field of irrigation could not be left untouched. But whatever the principles and policies, there was something very basic that the farmers expected of it.

For the farmers, an irrigation system is good if it delivers water on time in adequate quantities. Water released too early or too late to farm land and in volumes not required, be it less or more, is of no use. All irrigation projects in Nepal, especially the big ones, built through government initiative and international financial and technical inputs were started with the sole objective of providing water in time and in optimum volume. But the result is quite different.

However, the ideal level has been achieved by smaller farmer-managed irrigation systems where government intervention is little or nil. In contrast, the government-financed big irrigation projects, dictated in large measure by foreign consultants working for international aid agencies, have failed to deliver adequate water on time. Projects which are fairly functional have incurred heavy expenditure cost over the years, rendering them unsustainable.

This malaise is all the more unmistakable where India exercises control over water supply as, say, in the Koshi and Gandak projects. The water supply becomes irregular because the structures geared to Nepal are not properly maintained. The priority always goes to supplying water to the Indian canal system.

Particularly in the lean season, the Nepalese farmers are very much left high and dry.

Those at the tail-end of the canal system are the ones most affected by the unsteady water supply. It is not only caused by faulty design of the project and inadequate supply of water but also by overuse of water by the head-end farmers who are not well versed with how the system works.

So the tail-enders rather rightly consider the so-called facility as a mere drainage canal. Where it has worked with extra endeavour as in Chitwan it has cost the project more than the gains made from increased crop harvest. From a financial point of view, it is absolutely not cost-effective.

Whether the projects are good for the farmers or not, the government has to support them with adequate staff and administration overheads. It has proved a source of continued financial burden to the government. Attempts to involve the user farmers in the management have been far from fruitful because the farmers are instinctively pragmatic in approach. If the irrigation system is useful they will be willing to take over. But since most of them are deemed not so useful in times of need, the farmers avoid burning their fingers in such uneconomic ventures.

In the circumstances, the irrigation systems which have devoured umpteen millions are sitting like ducks wondering when the final blow will actually come.

◆

Chapter Seventy-Seven

Cheapest to Dearest

The Marsyangdi hydroelectric project is a classic example of how a project is publicly projected as the cheapest but turns out to be the dearest. To begin with, it was announced that the 69 MW project estimated to cost a meagre $21 million would produce electricity at the rate of $304 per kW, perhaps the lowest in the world. But as time went by and the issue gained fresh momentum, the estimates started escalating.

The second estimate was placed at $183 million, nine times more than the initial figure. The third estimate followed with greater vengeance hiking the figure to $228 million, a rise of 24%. The fourth and final costing came to $323.3 million, a further upswing by 41% over the previous figure. Ultimately, the production cost of the project stabilised at $4,685.5 per kW, perhaps the highest ever in the world.

Since it was the World Bank which was spearheading fund mobilisation, there was no dearth of resources. The total amount of $323.3 came through loans from several countries. The World Bank itself chipped in $107 million, Saudi Arabia approved a credit of $25 million, Kuwait $21 million and Germany $71.5 million. Nepal had to mobilise resources equivalent to $98.8 million.

Marsyangdi is a free-flowing project that precludes a concrete dam construction. It is located on the Marsyangdi river, a tributary of the Trisuli river which drains the Gandak basin in central Nepal. Located 110 km west of Kathmandu, it is accessible from Hetauda, Kathmandu and Pokhara. Started in 1982, it was completed in 1990.

The World Bank, in its appraisal report, defended this project as the cheapest solution to address Nepal's power problem. Allegedly, the bank considered several alternative projects but in the end Marsyangdi was declared 'still the cheapest' project of all. The most viable project talked about at that time, next to the Marsyangdi, was the Sapta Gandaki which the bank rejected purely on economic grounds. But a study undertaken by an independent professional body claimed that the Sapta Gandaki project was far cheaper than the Marsyangdi. However, it is widely suspected that the decision-makers opted for Marsyangdi for hidden benefits.

The charge that the estimates were inflated beyond imagination was vindicated on the conclusion of the project. About $45 million was left unused which means that funds in excess of the actual need were mobilised for extra commission. Nepal still pays, according to the terms of agreement with the World Bank, a commitment charge on this excess amount which was not disbursed.

Right before the project was accepted by the government and the donor agencies, a lot happened during the pre-feasibility, feasibility and detailed designing stages. To begin with, a German consulting firm made a pre-feasibility report on the basis of which a global tender was called to carry out the detailed feasibility report on the project. Although there were a number of tenders submitted by different agencies, it was awarded to the same company on the condition that it appoint as its local agent a person suggested by a high royal official and that he be paid a handsome commission. The deal was clinched and at the behest of the local agent, the surveyor hiked the price of the project enormously.

When the construction started, it got enmeshed in several scandals. There were two main contractors from China and Japan. They had accepted the tunnelling and the powerhouse construction works for a total amount of $21.8 million. But they made a claim of $233 million, ten times more than what had originally been agreed upon, on the grounds that they had to perform more work than had been stated in the contract documents. But the official report of the project showed the actual expenses per item of work was less than the original estimates. However that carried no meaning. The contractors sued Nepal at an arbitration court for compensation. After a long haggling between the Nepalese government and the contractors, an out of court settlement of $69 million compensation was negotiated. In this respect, the contractors were paid more than three times the original deal. It was believed that some remote hands were pulling the strings.

Being fully aware of how decisions were made in Nepal, the foreign agencies engaged in the project give preference to curry favour with the powers that be instead of delivering quality services. As a consequence, the design of the whole project was made, necessitating its continuous repair and maintenance after its handing over to the Nepalese government, costing Nepal more than $330 million until 1998.

◆

PART VI
Aid, Advice and Miscarriage

Chapter Seventy-Eight

Reeling Under Pressure

Nepal, a small country sandwiched between China and India, had from time immemorial been hosting migrants from the north as well as the south. The population of Nepal is made up of the Aryans moving up from the south and the Mongoloids coming down from the north. In a sense, Nepal has been a melting pot of all sorts of natives and migrants for centuries. The influx of refugees to Nepal in recent decades epitomises endless movement of people in distress, with shelter and survival being the primary motive.

When the Chinese overran Tibet in the late fifties, thousands of Tibetans fled their homeland. The Dalai Lama along with a huge number of followers took refugee in India. Nepal had its share of the Tibetan refugees in thousands. Some of them travelled further down to India and some went to overseas countries. Most of those who entered into Nepal from Tibet are doing relatively well.

When the Burmese government drove the foreigners out in the 1970s, a few thousand Nepalese who were engaged in farm lands since the end of the Second World War returned to Nepal. While in Burma they were poor; they arrived in Nepal a lot poorer. They were the incidental victims of an anti-India campaign that swept Burma at that time. However, over some decades since, Nepalese from Burma have been integrated into the national mainstream.

The influx of undeclared refugees from the Indian north-east continues even to this day. When the anti-foreigner movement engulfed Nagaland, Assam and other adjoining states of India, the main intention was to drive the Bangladeshi migrants out. But the

Nepalese farming there for decades together were not left alone either. Thousands left their permanent settlement and fled to Nepal. Although the eviction was a sustained one, the problem somehow did not catch world attention.

But when the Bhutanese of Nepalese extraction began arriving in hordes in the 1990s, the effect was immense. In a well-orchestrated policy of ethnic cleansing, the Bhutanese government terrorised the Nepalese settlers to force them to flee. Starting in 1990, the number of refugees from Bhutan peaked in 1992 with as many as 1,000 persons arriving every day. The influx continued in 1993 and 1994 too though in decreasing number. By the end of 1997, the refugee camps in Nepal recorded 93,500 Bhutanese refugees. Around 8,000 to 10,000 refugees are believed to be living elsewhere in Nepal.

One hundred thousand plus Bhutanese refugees are no doubt a big burden for a poor country like Nepal. Nepal sought international assistance in setting up refugee camps in the eastern part of the country. The United Nations High Commissioner for Refugees (UNHCR) took over the responsibility of co-ordinating all affairs relating to the seven camps dotted with 18,625 makeshift dwellings. A number of donor governments along with a dozen international non- governmental organisations have chipped in to keep the refugees alive.

Millions of dollars go into running the refugee camps every year. The UNHCR has already spent $20 million in five years. Another $5 million was spent in 1996. Maintenance alone costs millions every year. There must necessarily be a limit to the flow of resources and patience for the problem of repatriation of refugees to Bhutan.

Many rounds of official talks have been held between the Bhutanese and the Nepalese authorities to deal with this nagging problem. Bhutan is not quite ready to take its citizens back, mainly on the pretext that all of them are not Bhutanese nationals. Before accepting them back, Bhutan wants to screen the refugees to ascertain whether they are the genuine citizens of Bhutan. Nepal agreed to the idea but differences over screening methods persist between the two governments. Nepal wants to get out of the situation as soon as possible in view of the heavy economic, environmental and security issues. But Bhutan is in no hurry and has adopted all kinds of delaying tactics.

In fact, Bhutan has already achieved its objective of ethnic cleansing and therefore could not care less what happens to the refugees. Many believe Bhutan could not possibly have succeeded in terrorising its own citizens had there been no outside support, namely from the Indian government. Nepal and Bhutan share no common border. India is a transit country between Nepal and Bhutan. When the Bhutanese refugees fled Bhutan, India allowed them to travel to Nepal through its territory. But after a few years, when the same Bhutanese wanted to go back to their country, India prevented them with force. India has refused to get involved in this so-called 'bilateral' problem despite repeated requests from Nepal, which is tantamount to giving indirect support to Bhutan to maintain an inflexible position.

While the Bhutanese refugees languish in groping darkness, Nepal is reeling under tremendous socio-economic and security pressures.

◆

Chapter Seventy-Nine

The Flying Bull

The Resources Conservation and Utilisation Project (RCUP) was once a prestige project of the USAID-Nepal. It was a multifaceted integrated development program. An American firm called Southeast Consortium for International Development (SECID) was hired in 1980 to implement a project in central Nepal.

SECID in turn hired and flew a bunch of American consultants to Nepal. The group included a forester, a soil scientist, three 'catchment' advisers, a training specialist and a social scientist. The talent was no doubt diverse but not as integrated as the project demanded. The great consultants started fighting among themselves. The battle of wits spilled over to the local community. One consultant was singled out, recalled and packed home.

The mishap occurred as one of the advisers bedded down at the ancient palace in Gorkha instead of interacting with the villagers to understand their needs. He was more fascinated by the architectural beauty of the monument on a mountain top than his immediate responsibility of attending to the problem of rural development.

The resource conservation experts designed big houses with big halls that required long logs to serve as single-piece support beams. The tallest trees in the neighbouring alpine forest were cut down for appropriate timber. The conservation projects very ironically had an impact on resource destruction which the whole exercise was designed to stop.

It would have been less rankling had the 174 houses built in different parts of the mountain been properly used. After the project, however, they were left empty because of inconvenient locations. The houses are there to tell what their foreign assistance can actually deliver.

Topping the RCUP achievements list was the bull flown from the US for cross-breeding and genetic improvement of the Nepalese livestock. Unfortunately, the Nepalese cows could not take the big American bull because they are not physically strong enough to withstand the 'American onslaught'. The consultant flew back home, leaving the poor bull on the desolate banks of the river Daraundi completely companionless, and unable to satisfy itself biologically.

No wonder that an evaluation report prepared by the International Science and Technology Institute in 1985 declared the RCUP a disastrous phenomenon. The project was accused of not using any integrated or workable management strategy. The institute also charged the project with trying too many things over too large an area too quickly. In a nutshell, it declared the $27.5 million spent on the project a monumental waste.

The Nepalese mountains moreover have many exotic, high profile development projects. The second hill irrigation project was of this kind. Jointly funded by the Asian Development Bank and the World Bank, its aim was to upgrade the existing irrigation systems in four western districts of Nepal.

The feasibility survey was conducted by Louis Berger, an American agency, which was subsequently appointed as the principal executing consultant. A young American agricultural engineer was contracted to carry out the job. He was completely new to Nepal and did not relish the rough mountainous terrain. He operated from Kathmandu with four of his locally recruited consultants running to and fro.

Unfortunately for him, the irrigation authorities of Nepal could not stomach his overly expensive designs. The matter came to a head with the Asian Development Bank instituting an evaluation of the works done. The ADB found the designs too sophisticated as they not only ignored the existing irrigation systems, but also the farmers' actual needs. The designs were of course rejected and the consultant left in total frustration. In the course of this futile exercise, Nepal lost no less than Rs. 8 million.

◆

Chapter Eighty

A Concrete Experiment

Nepal and Switzerland have many things in common. Both are mountainous countries. Both have water resources. But they also have something uncommon. Switzerland is highly developed, rich, secure and sophisticated. Nepal on the other hand is backward, poor and innocuous. When Nepal talks about development it looks towards Switzerland and aspires to be like her. The Swiss are equally fascinated with Nepal. They get nostalgic about their past when they come face to face with Nepal and the Nepalese people. If they had not developed to the extent they have, would they not be as miserable as the Nepalese today? Perhaps yes, perhaps not.

The question is hypothetical rather than sentimental. But in reality, the Swiss have helped Nepal with some concrete aid packages which have left a deep imprint on the development of Nepal. The Nepalese, for example, learnt cheese-making from the Swiss. Before the Swiss came, Nepalese drank milk of yaks, cows, buffaloes and goats. They made ghee (clarified butter), extracting fat out of the milk for export to India. With the money thus made the villagers bought imported salt, clothes, matches, cigarettes and other household essentials. The economy of Nepal went on like this for centuries.

The Swiss taught the Nepalese how to make cheese. It took years before the Nepalese understood the importance of cheese. It took yet many more years before the Nepalese developed a taste for it. However they did eventually and today the cheese industry is a thriving one with popular demand ever rising. Similarly, the Swiss built mountain roads widely acclaimed as environment friendly. Of them, the road to Jiri, east of Kathmandu, is famous for its bends and little damage to the surrounding vegetation.

The Jiri road is about 110 km long, starting from Lamosangu along the Kathmandu-Kodari Highway that leads to Lhasa in Tibet. It goes across the Sunkosi river, climbs a mountain with serpentine gait, passes through Charikot, a place of historic and commercial importance, and heads towards Jiri an experimental centre for modern mountain agriculture, scientific animal husbandry and cheese-making. The Jiri road also facilitates the movement of tourists going to the Everest region.

However, in the latter part of the 1970s, after ten years of its construction, the road had a sizeable mishap. A bridge built on the Charnabati river was swept away by a flash flood. This led to a complete closure of traffic for some time. Since the Nepalese government could not afford to install a new bridge and restore traffic, the Swiss came rushing. But this time around they had something up their sleeves.

Restoring the bridge was a tough call but the Swiss did it pretty quickly. It was the repair of the damaged areas downstream that was the hard nut to crack. They took up the challenge and undertook an experiment with concrete. The 2 km long downstream area saw, as a consequence, a concrete edifice emerging at the cost of Rs. 800 million, equalling the entire cost of the 110 km long Jiri road.

The secret of the unprecedented flood lay in the lack of Swiss understanding of the importance of big boulders lying on the Charnabati river. They had crushed the boulders to produce gravel for road construction. The boulders always had a role to play in stabilising the environment as they prevented the gushing water from eroding the area. But once they were gone, the water had a free space to cause destruction.

So in order to discipline the river, the Swiss laid down a 1 km long concrete bed with thousands of sacks of cement and iron rods. They created numerous gigantic tripods each devouring 500 bags of cement. The whole area around the new bridge became a new world of concrete, resembling a fortress against a possible nuclear attack.

Such a monumental work could not possibly miss the prying eyes of the world media. The Swiss press reported it which created an uproar in the Swiss parliament where questions were raised such as why Swiss money was being squandered so callously in making a poor country like Nepal a guinea pig. The Swiss government expectedly defended the concrete experiment on the grounds that the expensive experiment could be useful to Switzerland one way or another. It argued it did not matter to Nepal because the money was a free gift. Moreover, the Nepalese do not understand the intricacies of such an engineering experiment in their country anyway.

◆

Chapter Eighty-One

Keep it a Secret

The Nepalese talk about increasing and decreasing dependence on foreign aid and that issue always triggers an animated debate. But nobody knows how much foreign aid is coming to Nepal. What the people know is the volume of foreign loans which stands at nearly $2.5 billion. The information dearth applies also to technical assistance, turnkey projects, financial and commodity grants. Is it necessary to keep all this a secret?

Under the technical assistance programme, experts are provided to Nepal for project studies, most of which lead to foreign loans. In such cases, the major part of the funds remains with the donors themselves. Japan and Germany mention neither the total amount involved nor the salaries and perks their experts draw. Americans disclose the lump sum of technical assistance but withhold information on individual salaries. The UNDP gives the financial breakdown of these programmes. The experts pay their income tax, if at all, to their home governments. However, it has been taken for granted that nearly 80% of the funds goes to the experts and the remaining 20% is often spent on equipment, vehicles, computers, etc. for their use.

The auditor general of Nepal routinely points out in his annual report the dearth of information on the matter. The AG finds the financial records relating to aid from international agencies and individual donor nations inadequate, confusing and misleading. All it can do is to call upon the government ministries to obtain necessary information on aid agreements concluded with different international organisations and donor countries. But the plea has fallen on deaf ears which means one cannot have a comprehensive picture of foreign assistance to Nepal, not to speak of its impact on Nepal's economy.

Similarly, the Commission of Investigation on Abuse of Authority (CM), the anti-corruption statutory body, has also expressed displeasure on the non-availability of information on foreign-aided turnkey projects. It has said that it is not only improper to deprive Nepalese authorities of information on such projects but also dangerous from the national security point of view to leave everything including the financial transactions, selection of contractors, monitoring, evaluation, etc. entirely to the donor agencies. For want of information, reasonable doubts have been cast and the question whether the resources allocated for a given project may have been used for purposes other than developmental remains unanswered. But this has had no bearing on the attitude of the donor nations and agencies.

The Nepalese parliament has taken an increased interest in making the global tendering system and financial deals transparent. The sovereign legislature has called upon the government to make it obligatory for all concerned to make public the names of the local commission agents and the money they make on this account. When the Ministry of Finance tried to carry out this parliamentary directive, the donor agencies flatly refused to oblige. Nepal had to bow down before the adamant donors who wanted to protect the commission agents at all cost.

The constitution has granted the Nepalese the right to information on matters of public concern. The issue came to a head at a Nepalese court of law when the government tried to deny information on the controversial hydro-power project called Arun III. Following the verdict of the Supreme Court, the Ministry of Water Resources made a few of the reports on this project accessible to the non-governmental organisations. The reports were too old to reveal the real status of the project proposal. The vital information that really mattered was however leaked through informal channels. It was the hitherto concealed information that later added much fuel to the public debate on the controversial project. The demise of the project is attributed to World Bank conditions which were beyond the comprehension of ordinary Nepalese citizens. But the unfolding of the critical information did not leave any room for regret in the public's mind. The project is on indefinite hold.

The Nepalese people in general have been made to believe that the foreign aid is the panacea for all their economic ills. But they are at a loss to grasp how and to what extent it is doing any good to them. For want of proper information, there is no way they can challenge the claims all secretive donors make. Following close on the donors' heels, the government officials suspiciously endorse what the donors do. If nothing is wrong in disseminating information, why fear? The fact that the information is kept confidential makes one conjecture that something may indeed be wrong.

◆

Chapter Eighty-Two

The Heavy String

Donor countries and agencies extend loans to Nepal for big development projects with some strings attached - of course. One of the so-called strings is the provision for international technical consultancy. The credit agreement includes a provision under which an international consultancy agency is to be hired for the implementation, supervision, monitoring and evaluation of the project. The consultant's fee is incorporated in the loan agreement. In other words, Nepal has to bear the high fee paid to international consultants.

Being at the receiving end, Nepal has very little, if any, say in the selection of the international consultants although it participates in the selection process. In the case of a drinking water project, the lowest bidder ran short by just a few months in meeting the stipulated period of professional experience. The fee difference between the lowest and the second lowest bidder was something like Rs. 70 million.

The Nepalese government wanted to hire the lowest bidder on grounds that a few months' experience was immaterial in this case. Look at the amount of money that can be saved, said the Nepalese officials. The donor agency did not budge an inch from its stand. Finally, the donor agency prevailed and Nepal lost a cool Rs. 70 million.

Left to itself, Nepal can and will never pay an exorbitant fee of $30,000 to $35,000 per month to a consultant. Not only is the figure an insult to poverty-stricken Nepal but also daylight robbery. The great consultant could never dream of making that much dough in his own 'industrialised' society. But since this is a take it or leave it proposal, Nepal concedes with a heavy heart. Nonetheless the groans are heard all over the country. The auditor general's office which has an insight into the performance of international consultants has often made no secret of its discontent.

The auditor general has established that projects implemented under the supervision of the international consultants have been delayed, incurring phenomenal extras in the total project outlay. Also found objectionable is the practice of these consultants sub-contracting works without prior consultation with the host government. This also contributes to cost escalation. The consultants have also been found guilty of arbitrarily changing the suppliers of materials and equipment for extra money. They were also found guilty of making payments without verifying documents properly.

The gravest of the charges laid against the international consultants relates to the poor quality of work completed under their supervision. Although they have been held responsible for defective construction, they are not considered legally accountable. In other words, the consultants perform a job for which they are not held accountable. So the losses stemming from their faults and misjudgements have to be borne by the host country. The auditor general has hinted at foul play on several fronts. In project implementation, for example, the consultants extend the term of the contractors which necessitates prolonging their own term with the result that the project cost escalates by many times.

Taking cue from these comments, the Public Accounts Committee of parliament asked the government to formulate a fair and uniform norm for the execution of foreign-aided projects under the supervision of international consultants. But the government has not, rather could not, act on it for obvious reasons. Utter helplessness characterises Nepal's mindset vis-a-vis international loan agreements.

The Commission on Investigation on Abuse of Authority (CIAA) has also taken note of this weird phenomenon during its investigation of alleged misuse of foreign funds in rural drinking water schemes. The commission deemed it incongruous for the small drinking water projects in the village to hire foreign consultants when technicians of equal calibre and competence were available in Nepal itself

Perfectly avoidable waste of national resources on foreign expertise has also been duly recorded. The CIAA wonders if this kind of waste in money and manpower would not encourage a brain drain. A whole new look on extraneously funded projects is strongly recommended. Is anybody listening? Even though there may be somebody listening, nobody seems in a position to break the vicious circle that international aid money has created in Nepal.

◆

Chapter Eighty-Three

A Million-Dollar Gate

Ever heard of a million dollar gate in a poor country like Nepal?
That's what makes even a reality unreal in Nepal. The kind of gate
that has been conceived is of course a mundane one but the location
is rather intriguing. Actually it is a device to drain out water from
a glacial lake which is believed to be on the brink of implosion - an
imminent threat to life and property. Whether such an expensive
gate needs to be built or will ever be built is something quite
incomprehensible to the people of Nepal. But how international
resources flow in for such dubious purposes indicates the mystery
that surrounds international aid.

Chho Rolpa is a glacial lake in the eastern Himalayas. It was
feared that it would burst and sweep away habitation downstream.
In the summer of 1997, panic gripped the area from the mountains
to the plains, with the potential threat of a flash flood from the lake.
The government in fact evacuated people living immediately
below the glacier and sounded an alert to all whose lives were
under threat.

As the issue heightened public interest as well as fear,
national and international experts debated the pros and cons of the
two schools of thought that had emerged. One group pointed out
the implosion of the glacial lake was imminent whereas the other
group ruled that out. Irrespective of the debate's nature, action on
preventive measures was very much on the cards.

Simple as it may have appeared at the start, it was later
discovered that the whole hullabaloo was motivated by the desire
to have a project proposal approved by the government of the
Netherlands. The project was worth Rs. 150 million ($2.5 million).

The trick worked because the Dutch government did indeed approve the project which was pending for several years following the alarm sounded within and without Nepal. The glacier remains calm as ever before except that a lot of resources have come and gone in its name.

The project was meant basically to drain the water from the lake to reduce the extent of damage in the event an implosion really took place. For this purpose, four gates each measuring 5 metres in length have been proposed. The whole idea is self-contradictory because it is not aimed at redressnig the threat posed by this glacier. It only tries to minimise the impact of the predicted damage downstream.

According to estimates, there is currently 80 million cubic metres of water in the lake. To make it danger-free, the water level should be reduced by 20 metres, but the proposal plans to reduce it by only 3 metres by means of an artificial drainage system. This will be effective only for two to three years, after which the lake would revert to its original shape. In other words, the threat, imagined or real, will return after that period.

Whatever the actual situation, the project will be over and its fund used. How it will be used is worth probing into. Out of $2.5 million, $1.9 million will be used in the construction of four drainage gates and the rest ($600,000) will go to an international consultant who is a British national. The gates' construction will need only 288 bags of cement and 15 tonnes of iron rods. But the cement and the iron rods are to be transported by helicopters, the cost of which will be over $1 million. For air tickets alone, $40,000 has been allocated. The consultant who will be engaged in the project only for two months is to spend three weeks in the field and be paid $600,000.

◆

Chapter Eighty-Four

Extraordinary Expertise

Nepal is seen as a lucky country, flooded as it is by international aid from both known and unknown sources to alleviate poverty and deprivation. People tend to use the term 'alleviation' and not 'elimination' of poverty. Perhaps none of them believes that the problem can ever be eliminated. Or else they wish to keep poverty uneliminated because it serves as a playground for development players, national as well as international. Whatever the reasons, Nepal provides a fertile ground for all the kinds of experiments one can think of

Way back in 1982, an international organisation called the Worldview International Foundation (WIF) was established in Kathmandu to bring about a revolution in the communication sector. There was no television in the country. Worldview saw an excellent opportunity to make its presence felt in Nepal by offering professional training to the pioneers of Nepal Television (NTV) which was finally commissioned in 1985. The WIF virtually had a free hand in NTV affairs.

Nepal is sold for a price that it never gets. The middleman always bags the lion's share of the price. Nepal was one of the three Asian beneficiaries in an interesting project designed to build communications capacity for environmentally sustainable development. The other two countries were Thailand and Malaysia. It was a project with an outlay of $1.5 million granted by NORAD. Worldview International was the project-executing organisation. The amount was allocated thus: Thailand and Malaysia around $400,000 each, Nepal $380,000 and the remaining $320,000 was set aside for the co-ordinating executing organisation.

But in actuality, what was disbursed was $150,000 each to the three countries, which is only 30% of the total fund made available by NORAD.

Worldview Nepal, which has been in operation since 1982 with an excellent professional and financial record, was on the brink of collapse in 1996 due, among other factors, to funding drought. Had it received $380,000 as allocated during the original project formulation, it could have had a smooth sailing for more than a decade contributing continuously to professional development of broadcasting in Nepal. Sadly though, the prosperity of the WIF bigwigs mattered more than the interests of the poor institution at the receiving end.

The misuse of 70% of the resources under this project, amounting to $1,050,000, by the intermediary headquarters was not only unbearable but also in direct contravention of the contract signed with NORAD. The irony was that the implementing agencies, namely the national chapters of the WIF, were reeling under a financial crunch while bigwigs seated at the headquarters were misappropriating the funds allocated for achieving specific training targets in designated countries. According to the original schedule of resource distribution, the recipient nations were to get 78% of the NORAD grant. But it was juggled upside down and the HQ bosses ended up consuming 70% of the fund. It may not surprise anybody if the brokers got a piece of the pie. What was astonishing was how the donor agency, NORAD, was convinced by the account-keeping which was a miracle.

◆

Chapter Eighty-Five

An Itinerant Crusader

This is a story of a crusader from Norway, who took unto himself the horrendous job of starting the poor countries of Asia and Africa on a modern communication revolution. He has imagination, powers of persuasion and physical tenacity to run all over the world with a hold-all that enables him to check in as the last passenger and check out as the first one in airports. What a wonderful man he is! He can raise millions of dollars over a phone call. He is a jet-setter who spends eleven months of the year on international travel. His family gets just one month of his time in a year during Christmas.

Small wonder he was able to create over a span of two decades an independent organisation known as the Worldview International Foundation (WIF) which is headquartered in Colombo with national chapters splashed over several countries in Asia and Africa. He envisions a thriving network of national organisations with a mission to use the communication tool to revolutionise, reform and restructure Third World societies. He nearly succeeded with sheer strength of his personal involvement and dedication.

But he has his Achilles' heel - administration. With all his virtues and vices, he became the Hindu trinity - the creator, the sustainer and the destroyer. He created WIF chapters in Nepal, Sri Lanka, Bangladesh, Thailand, Malaysia, the Maldives and Syria. He even expanded WIF wings to African countries like Botswana, Kenya, and Tanzania. There is no doubt the 'great' guy sustained all these organisations mainly through his personal charm. The trouble is that the moment he disengages himself from the self-engineered monolith everything will collapse like a house of cards.

The annual report of his organisation showed a turnover of $2 to $3 million. That, however, is meant only for public consumption. The fiscal allocations are technically approved by what is called the General Body, a rubber stamp as far as budgetary matters are concerned. How the annual budget gets endorsed presents an interesting case scenario. The finance chief distributes a rough balance sheet to the General Body and grants just fifteen minutes for comments and questions. Before a member is finished browsing through the document, the time is declared over and the budget stands unanimously endorsed. If ever somebody raises a point of doubt, the boss thunders back as if his personal integrity has been questioned. No one dares to 'displease' the boss.

In one instance, a fund of around $300,000 from the Netherlands was included in the budget. But wonder of wonders, not a single penny of it was channelled through the official accounting system. The fund was from the Dutch government, for a Dutch consultant. It was indeed a unique fund which trained one person each from fifteen countries of Asia in video production. The report claimed that this training had helped revolutionise the audio-visual component of the communication system in Thailand, Malaysia, Sri Lanka and India.

Two trainees from Nepal have never touched a video camera since, nor are they engaged in any way in this profession. One was a scholar and another an officer in some establishment. But $300,000 continues to flow from the Dutch treasury. The tailpiece, as it were, is that the Worldview boss is still elated that the Dutch government is providing the free grant in the name of the poor countries, an act that enables him to adorn his financial reports with big impressive figures.

◆

Chapter Eighty-Six

Holiday Production

An actress could be famous and popular in Norway but that does not mean a thing in a strange country like Nepal. The Worldview boss who met the actress casually at some social gathering decided to make her play a meaningful role in society. She was given the responsibility to train young Nepalese video producers on script conceptualisation, research, writing and refining. She came, she met a group of youngsters, and started her lessons. Unfortunately, she spoke Norwegian English which was beyond the trainees' comprehension. She liked Nepal, its friendly people, mild weather and respect for humanity. Evidently these features were wanting in her home country.

She wanted to produce a film, something that she had never done before. Back home she was acting in some low-grade films so understandably the company could spare her for any length of time. She was again back in Nepal for a longer stay. She went through fairy tales, legends and myths of Nepal but none appealed to her as a potential theme for the film of her dream. Finally, she settled down with a story on the destiny of man. She titled the film upon return to Norway, as though the theme dealt with the duty of man, not the destiny of man.

The change in title can be traced to her distrust of the Nepalese who had worked with her for several months together. When a technical problem occurred during film production she faxed a message to Oslo to check if the Nepalese technicians were telling the truth or taking her for a ride. Over a period of three months, the fax messages piled up so much that it cost the Nepalese agency concerned as much money as one would spend on a man travelling to and from Norway.

Her distrust of the Nepalese was heightened whenever the Nepalese talked in their native language in front of her. She thought something was being said against her. She even went to extent of demanding that everybody spoke in English before her. She was getting quite unbearable but nobody wanted to offend or hurt her because she was a guest.

The WIF paid for the hotel room but she insisted on staying at the guest room in the office. She started becoming sick with contaminated water and food. Yet she refused to shift to a decent hotel nor would she agree to go to a hospital for treatment. She suffered from excessive diarrhoea, a common ailment in Kathmandu, and had fainting fits. Once in the middle of the night she had to be rushed to the hospital for emergency treatment, but she defied the doctor's advice to remain there. She said she could take care of herself which she obviously could not. From time to time, she had to be taken to the hospital for this or that problem.

Solid food is avoided and plenty of glucose given when a person is struck by diarrhoea. In her case, it was not possible as she was allergic to sugar. Doctors were consulted on how to cure her. She would not listen to them. Again she faxed messages to Oslo seeking advice on her treatment. A simple ailment was being made too complicated. Her suspicious nature quite simply disregarded local medical advice. She complained that she was not taken good care of and naturally her colleagues were deeply hurt by her statement.

It was in the professional field of directing, producing and editing the film, though, that she got thoroughly exposed. She had all along been claiming, and as it turned out, feigning, to know what she did not. That apart, she had no previous experiences worth the name. She has a crew of excellent cameramen, an editor, assistant director, and actors and actresses, arguably the best Nepal could offer. As she was the monarch of all she surveyed everybody had to unlearn something of what they had learnt before. She often went crazy, driving others in the same direction.

At the editing room she absolutely betrayed her poverty of mind. She could not decide what to retain and what to chop. For a fifteen-minute film, some eighty hours were allotted but it was doubled simply because she was completely ignorant of professional as well as thematic matters. The editor would finally lose patience and throw her out of the room to give himself the time and concentration to finish the job

After all was said and done, she was still unsatisfied with the product. She asked, upon her return home, for all the cassettes to be sent to Oslo. What happened then? The final product was completely distorted and disfigured. The film never saw the light of day in Nepal. Did it ever matter to anybody? No. Wasn't it, after all, a holiday trip taken for a holiday production?

◆

and concentrated to finish the job.

After all was said and done, she was "cumulatively and in private" asked, upon her return home, about the chances to be saved in Oslo. What happened next? The final bid had been completely discarded and distributed. No one really knew. By noon of any or either bids distributed, or nine by ninety's worth, or TE after all. A standard turndown for a nascent provision.

Poison Prevention 243

Chapter Eighty-Seven

Poisoning Advice

To get pesticide for increased agricultural output, Nepal needed foreign consultants who were aplenty. Over the last forty years, innumerable foreign experts have promoted the use of pesticides besides chemical fertilisers. Today, Nepal needs to get rid of the tonnes of pesticide as they pose health hazards to the people living near the stockpiles of them.

The most glaring example of this highly poisonous stockpile is noticed in Amlekhgunj along a highway, some 200 km south of Kathmandu. Fifty tonnes of pesticide wait there, serving as the Mecca for poison consultants from different parts of the world. Distinguished visitors went there from New Zealand, Finland and several other countries.

In between their visits, the villagers have fallen victims to the poison. As many as twenty-seven villagers in the neighbourhood have already died of poisoning. Skin disease is a common phenomenon. The kala-azar (black fever) has taken the major toll. The local livestock have not been spared. The villagers are of course angry but they are helpless to do anything about it. Because it is a poison that needs to be done away with, you need to bury it underground, you need experts to burn it in extraordinary fire and you need experts to pour down water on the fire.

To use pesticide you can easily make do with lowly paid technicians but to destroy it you need very highly paid and foreign experts because Nepal has no expertise to handle or play with chemical poisons.

The United Nations Development Programme and the Asian Development Bank came forward with help in 1989 and spent

$577,000 on the exercise. A New Zealand agency was contracted to take care of the stockpile of poison and indeed 144 tonnes of less dangerous pesticide was got rid of through reprocessing, refining, spreading and burying processes. The more dangerous portion was to be burned in the cement factory, not far from the site of the stockpile. But the news started a panic throughout the area, forestalling the proposed destruction.

Then came a master plan in 1997 for the destruction of the said pesticide with assistance from the Asian Development Bank. The plan recommended a special commission to supervise the training of technical personnel and to procure necessary public-safety equipment. The final disposal has been scheduled for the year 2000. In the meantime, the plan recommends strict vigilance, regular monitoring, repackaging, maintaining cleanliness, etc. After destruction an assessment of all the effects on the environment has been recommended. A few more millions of dollars would be required to procure foreign equipment and hire foreign consultants.

Finland is trying to help Nepal with all necessary resources and expertise. Nepal has signed the international convention on shipment of dangerous chemicals at the behest of Finland. According to the work plan, of second and third-generation pesticides would be destroyed in isolated places, away from human settlements. High-voltage electric cables would be avoided. Some pesticide would be burnt in the furnace of the cement factory where temperature ranges from 1200 to 2000 degrees centigrade.

If nothing else, 10 tonnes of mercury is causing a big headache to the people dealing with this blessing-turned-bane chemical. Since Finland has the necessary facility to destroy it without any ill effects, the mercury awaits transportation to Scandinavia. Or, it may have to be transported to United States or some European countries where a suitable facility exists. There is also a German plant in Mumbai in India, where some kinds of pesticide can be destroyed.

Amlekhgunj is not the only place where pesticide poison has been dumped. A depot in Khumaltar in Kathmandu itself, belonging to the agriculture department has about two trucks of poison which have been lying dormant for over twenty-five years. It contains twelve cylinders of a dangerous chemical called methyl bromide. Similarly, there is a government store in the heart of Nepalgunj, 300 km west of Kathmandu, which houses 2,300 litres and 8 tonnes of powder pesticide. A little further to the west in Bardia, there are 10,000 litres of similar poison dumped in the warehouse of the cotton crop project. There is an unknown amount of DDT in many parts of Nepal.

The pesticide came to Nepal either as a free gift or was obtained under the recommendation of the international consultants to bolster agricultural production. The imported volume of pesticide could not be consumed as the procurement was in excess of the actual needs. The bigger the quantity, the bigger the commission. Now it has become a national threat, for the redress of which international help is being sought. Before it is taken care of, it is sure that many people will lose their lives and many properties will be damaged by the poisonous fallout.

◆

Chapter Eighty-Eight

Makaimara Tricks on McNamara

An Israeli consultant was a pervasive character in a rural development project in the Rasuwa and Nuwakot districts of Nepal. His claim to fame was that he had once churned out a paper on women's development and empowerment in Africa. Otherwise he had no clue whatsoever about Nepali culture, less still his own professional obligation. However, he was great in the art of plagiarism. Borrowing ideas from a Nepalese scholar's paper without offering any attribution, the consultant in question landed himself a job in Nepal and a lucrative one at that. If it were in the US, he would have been appropriately penalised for deceiving his employer. Anything goes in Nepal, plagiarism not excluded.

His primary duty was to help the villagers to increase farm output with improved seeds. As was his wont, he instead concentrated in following his basic instinct - fooling around with women. Open advocating: 'No married life is better than a married life of a bachelor', he undoubtedly had the best five years of his life in Nepal. He went home with half a million dollars out of the total project cost of $8 million provided by the World Bank in the form of a soft loan. A few times he tried to help the farmers by supplying improved maize seeds, but somehow, to his misfortune, the seeds never germinated.

The villagers were furious with him but that did not do him any harm. On the contrary, he was rewarded by no less a person than Robert McNamara himself, then the World Bank President, who had reportedly intervened seventeen times to retain him on the job even though Nepal had asked for his dismissal on grounds of incompetence and ineptitude. To his good fortune, McNamara visited Nepal to inspect the World Bank-funded projects. The Bank boss flew to Rasuwa- Nuwakot area where this consultant was assigned. During exactly three minutes of briefing by the consultant, all other officials and villagers were cleverly kept at arm's length. McNamara went back to Washington DC with the erroneous impression that food availability in the region covered by the project had indeed increased.

The villagers later fretted and fumed at the lies fed to McNamara but the die, as it were, had already been cast. The farmers nicknamed McNamara's consultant 'Makaimara' (the Nepalese equivalent for the killer of the maize crops). The term 'Makaimara' figured in the World Bank documents also for some period but that did not change McNamara nor the consultant's status and fortune.

Under another World Bank loan programme, a British adviser based in Washington DC came flying to Nepal. He stayed at a five-star hotel in Kathmandu for two months and produced a report on the rural development strategy for Nepal. Nepal's Ministry of Finance where the said report was submitted forwarded the document to the National Planning Commission for approval. It was very obediently endorsed and later circulated to members of the Nepal Aid Group for resource mobilisation.

Unfortunately the great document did not have a smooth sailing as the Nepalese government had already manufactured a home-grown rural development strategy. This indigenous idea of making the elected representatives the main fulcrum of local planning and development conflicted with the top-down planning process recommended by the World Bank adviser, who happened to be a British bureaucrat retired from what was called the Indian Civil Service during the colonial era.

When the Nepalese government shot down his idea, he got furious and called on the World Bank to suspend all assistance to Nepal. He obviously had not shrugged off his colonial hangover one bit. He thought he alone had the authority to formulate policy for a poor and backward Nepal. All that the Nepalese government was supposed to do was execute obediently what he had thought best for Nepal. As he failed to see his recommendation through, he assumed a vindictive posture throughout the time he was in the World Bank's payroll.

◆

Chapter Eighty-Nine

Trading Adviser

During the heyday of rural development wave in Nepal, a huge project worth Rs. 450 million was launched in the districts of Siraha, Saptari and Udaypur in Nepal's southeastern Terai. A calculation says that the project spent Rs. 250,000 per day for five years to eat up the allocated fund. The Asian Development Bank had extended a loan for the project and, as usual, a handsomely paid adviser from Sri Lanka was given the job of overseeing the project implementation.

It was a godsend assignment for him and he wanted to make the best possible use of the opportunity not only to make money but also to enjoy life at the end of his life. Before his arrival in Nepal, he married a young girl who looked his granddaughter's age, leaving his first wife behind at home. He made certain he had a luxurious apartment and a mammoth Japanese Landcruiser for use during trips to the project areas which were some 300 km east of Kathmandu.

Had he confined himself to his lovely wife, pretty apartment and sleek foreign vehicle (his salary was $100,000 per annum) nobody in Nepal would have cared. But he went a step too far. Though the gentleman hardly ever visited the project areas to grapple with the issues involved, he frequently embarked on trips to his favourite destination - Raxaul, an Indian border town.

His goal was to buy lots and lots of Indian textiles and other consumer items as much as his sturdy four-wheel drive machine could take. Whatever he bought was meant for shipment to Sri Lanka. Indian textiles are in high demand in Sri Lanka, as are other consumer items, but the supply is restricted. No quantitative restriction has been placed on the importation of Indian goods to Nepal. Goods purchased in the Indian border town are cheaper than in Nepal as that would avoid Nepalese duty on them. That is the reason why he frequented Raxaul.

He openly suggested to his staff and subordinates in the projects to buy all goods required in the project from a particular firm in Kathmandu. In Nepal it is a normal practice to give some commission on all purchases, especially the ones relating to a government office. The consultant could not care less about consequences as he felt very secured in the job as an international expert.

His abrasiveness was unmistakable when it was discovered that he was carrying two registration plates for his vehicle - a white one (government vehicle) for normal days and a red (private vehicle) for the weekends and public holidays. Because of widespread misuse of government vehicles, the government had restricted vehicle use only to official working days and so at weekends the adviser decided to replace the white plate with a red one for free movement. The matter was reported to the police but somehow he escaped and was never caught red-handed.

To justify his non-existent visit to the field, the adviser once reported to his headquarters that as there was no drainage system at Lahan, a small town, the place was blocked on account of waterlogging. By so saying, he wanted to impress upon his Manila-based superiors that his familiarity with the area was impeccable. Besides, he wanted to demonstrate his concern for the success of the project. The ADB showed equal amount of concern by heeding his message and promptly sought information from the Nepalese government. The Nepalese government sent its officers to inspect the reported flood in Lahan. To their surprise, the flood was nowhere visible. The matter was of course immediately reported to the ADB in Manila. The adviser was caught off guard.

By now it was crystal clear that the Sri Lankan gentleman was too busy with his personal agenda to give even an iota of attention to project activities. When the Nepalese government decided that he was not good enough, it asked for his recall. Subsequently he was made to pack up. He had barely completed one and a half years of his five-year assignment. The episode, however, created a furore on the international aid circuit. The opinion seemed to suggest that throwing an expatriate adviser out is something a poor county like Nepal need not have dared.

The Nepalese press broke the news about the recall. It was picked up by international wire services. A storm of sorts was caused in the teacup in some Asian capitals. The Sri Lankan ambassador to India, who was accredited to Nepal also at that time, called on Nepal's Foreign Ministry. At the envoy's request a full account was demanded from the Ministry of Local Development that directly dealt with the project. It took some weeks before the dust really settled. Nevertheless, the adviser was out of Nepal thankfully before any of his 'advice' was tested in the field.

◆

Chapter Ninety

Artificial Limbs

Decentralisation is a hot cake in Nepal. Currently it is a pet slogan for one and all who are in power. Be it real democracy, pseudo-democracy or whatever, decentralisation is the dominant theme. In its name, one proposes and the other disposes. But the process goes on regardless. It does not matter if it is bottom-up or top-down or somewhere in the middle. Cashing in on the great enthusiasm of the Nepalese to decentralise and devolve power to the grass roots, the UNDP jumped in the fray with an innovative idea.

UNDP manufactured a scheme to let itself intervene in the decentralisation process, without being accountable should the idea flounder midway. A device has been put together to ensure that the national exercise of transferring power to the local bodies occurs with the world body getting all the credit. But should the process fall, nobody would be in a position to point a finger at it.

The scheme under review is the brainchild of an American rural development adviser. It proposed that a bunch of 'officers' be sent to district-level organisations, formally called the District Development Committees (DDCs). Nepal has seventy-five districts covering some 4,000 villages. The DDC serves as a link between the centre and the villages. Under this scheme, the UNDP deputes a group of people to help the DDCs in planning, social development, communication, agriculture, education, health, etc. Work is not their mandate; they are there to pressurise the DDCs to expedite works that the district-level agencies of the government are supposed to be doing.

One exemplary service they provide is to help build up a data bank on different sectors under the purview of local development as a programme. The agricultural officer made an amazing forecast that the district he was assigned to would produce 7,500 tonnes of maize in 1998. To make such a forecast is no small deal even in Nepal. Later the officer demystified his own wisdom by clarifying that he had just added 5% growth to the previous year's production record.

The UNDP presence firmed up on the basis of these 'officers' already covers twenty districts. It is in the process of being expanded to twenty more districts. Having got the power to hire and fire the officers superimposed in Nepal's indigenous administrative mechanism, the 'officers' are fast becoming a part of the government without really belonging to it. So the critics of the project aptly describe the approach as a programme by the UNDP, of the UNDP and for the UNDP.

Yet another good example of how the UNDP is turning into an implementing agency from a funding agency in Nepal is testified by a programme called the GEF (Global Environmental Facility). The fund comes from the World Bank, and the UNDP is the executing agency. The whole objective of the programme is to encourage indigenous non-governmental organisations to carry out grass-roots activities for environmental protection and nature conservation. A local NGO named NEFEJ (Nepal Forum of Environmental Journalists) was selected to co-ordinate and disburse $100,000 to environmentally oriented local independent bodies.

The selection was done in a very transparent way through an open competition supervised by local experts and activities. Out of two hundred and fifty applicants about one hundred were selected to receive funds for small projects. This program actually set in motion a process of nationwide mobilisation of community-based organisations towards enhanced environmental awareness and protection measures. A few lapses were inevitable but the major part of the resources was used in a satisfactory way.

That was precisely what the UNDP could not stomach. When the second phase of the GEF arrived, the UNDP kept the whole business very close to its chest. Instead of bringing it to public notice the UNDP decided to handle the available resources on its own. The UNDP officials encouraged their henchmen and cronies to set up NGOs, which is not at all a difficult task thanks to the freedom enjoyed by organisations. The UNDP granted all the money to these hand-picked organisations. The very purpose of the

GEF, that is to induce wider participation of the environmental organisations, was defeated. But it could not care less because its glossy pamphlets can always justify its decision, no matter how unwise and authoritarian.

◆

Chapter Ninety-One

Symbol of Secrecy

The Bagmati bridge links Kathmandu with Patan city. Since these two cities are physically integrated, even though managed by separate municipalities, the bridge is indispensable to the mass transit of pedestrians as well as public transportation. The phenomenal growth in the population of these towns owing to migration rather than natural births has imposed added traffic pressure. At one point the traffic was so heavy that the old bridge caved in. The problem was further exacerbated by extraction of sand from the basement of the bridge for new constructions. For several months the whole traffic had to be diverted to a makeshift pontoon bridge over the Bagmatl river before a new bridge was installed.

While the old bridge was pulled up to set it right on a firmer foundation, a new bridge appeared beside the old one. Japan had offered to construct the new one, a proposal Nepal could not refuse. Some Japanese engineers and technicians came to Nepal and in no time the bridge emerged in all its glory. Impressed by the fast pace of construction, some got curious about the cost which nobody knew. Being a turnkey project, a free gift from Japan, no question could be asked, nor was Japan obliged to furnish replies. Cost, therefore, was immaterial.

But that led to a furious guessing game for the Nepalese officials and engineers who took a rather distant professional interest in the project. Some said the cost was Rs. 660 million while others surmised it was Rs. 260 million. Those engaged in the guessing game included officials of the Auditor General's Office and the Ministry of Transport and the members of the Public

Accounts Committee of the parliament. If they had no idea who else would?

However, the Public Accounts Committee was bent on finding out the cost for its records. The government started, on its prompting, making enquiries through proper channels. After six months, it was revealed that the cost calculation was almost complete but no information could be divulged. Perhaps it will never be known, as Japan could not care less about Nepal's sensitivities. A donor, after all, is a donor.

Going by their experience, the Nepalese engineers said that based on current price, the said bridge could be built at Rs. 100 to 120 million. Based on this calculation, at least two to five similar bridges could be built with the same 'mysterious' volume of resources expended on the single bridge. Missed opportunities do not count in the world of international aid, shrouded as it always is by mystery after mystery.

The Bagmati bridge is a symbol of donor secrecy which is a common feature in all turnkey projects. The Nepalese government has no control over them. After an agreement with the host government, the donor country carries out the works through its own chosen agency, procures all necessary equipment itself and hires the manpower likewise. The Nepalese government figures only at project handing-over ceremonies. The agreement mentions the total outlay of the project but the Nepalese government does not know if that amount had actually been spent, how it was spent and what happens to the deficits incurred or savings made.

The auditor general of Nepal has time and again complained about the mystery surrounding foreign assistance in terms of cash, kind or technology. He has come face to face with instances where the records of the fund-approving agencies and the line ministries do not tally, rendering proper auditing impossible. There are several other examples where the donor agencies use money which is not listed in official documents of the government. It has detected more than Rs. 2.4 billion as being unaccounted for. One can easily imagine how an unaudited account can be manipulated or misused. Donors' intransigence, many argue, is the major stumbling block on the way to evolving a transparent administrative culture in Nepal.

Instances abound where the donor agencies back down from their commitment to finance development activities. According to a practice followed in aid disbursement, the Nepalese government has to spend the money on a given project and then request for reimbursements from the donors. The donor agencies can find a thousand and one faults in the project and refuse to abide by its commitment. In 1997 alone, the government was stung for Rs. 718 million. In fact, the resources are wasted as the project as such is left in midstream for want of funds from either the government or the funding agencies.

◆

Chapter Ninety-Two

Leaving in the Lurch

Gurkhas are brave but they are poor. Since they are poor they join the army, preferably foreign. Judged against objective facts, the Gurkhas' first preference is the British army and then the Indian army and only then the national army.

The poor Gurkhas got a rude shock when Britain announced the decision to phase out the Gurkha regiment following the transfer of Hong Kong to China in 1997. They were in for yet another shock when they discovered how paltry their retirement benefits were.

A rifleman, for example, earned British £784 per month while on active service. On retirement, though, he was entitled to only £25 per month. After certain deductions, the take-home falls down to £14. That is not enough even to meet his bare minimum living expenses.

The situation got aggravated further when the pension went on decreasing as a result of rapid devaluation of the Nepalese rupee against the British pound. It was caused by the fact that the pension was erroneously fixed in terms of the Nepalese currency instead of the British pound.

To cite an example, a recruit got about £36 in 1987 when £1 fetched Rs. 35. But the same person received only £13 when the exchange rate was Rs. 103. So the British Gurkhas demanded that their pension be quoted in pounds sterling. Their voices went unheard.

Apart from this practical adjustment, the point where the Gurkhas feel very hurt is the discriminatory treatment on matters of pension compared to their British counterparts. The Tripartite Agreement signed by the UK, India and Nepal under which the

Nepalese boys are permitted to serve in the British and Indian armies spells out equity in terms of financial benefits. But it is here that the Gurkhas have been left in the lurch.

Let us take an example of a Gurkha soldier. He is entitled to a pension of about £24 after fifteen years of service. But a British soldier under similar circumstance is entitled to £256. Even after tax deductions, an ex-British soldier is left with a take-home of £171. It is seven times more than a Gurkha makes. Similarly, in the case of an officer, the difference is ten times. A Gurkha officer gets £33 whereas a British officer walks off with £315 pounds.

The Gurkhas upon their return home have organised what they call the ex-servicemen associations. They have humbly and only at times obstreperously raised their voice to claim the attention of the Nepalese and the British governments to the legitimacy of the issues involved. The Gurkhas are not aspiring to a standard of living equal to their British counterparts. The issue is that the amount given is not even enough to sustain minimum Nepalese standards. Indeed the matter was taken up at the highest levels of both governments. Consequently the British government gave an assurance to attend to this Gurkha grievance. After two years, the British government acted but offered only peanuts that the Gurkhas rejected outright.

Apart from those legally entitled to pensions, there are thousands of soldiers who are deprived of a regular pension. They are the ones who fought alongside Allied forces in the Second World War but were packed off home with a paltry severance pay. The number of such soldiers in Nepal is estimated to be 11,000. The welfare grant they get is given only after a cumbersome process of screening is completed. But it is claimed that the so-called Gurkha Appeal Fund from which these grants are made is much fatter than it is made out to be. This fund was generously contributed to by the Europeans after the Second World War. How big it actually is and what part of it is being used for the Gurkhas' welfare is a jealously guarded secret with the British government.

The other grey area in the financial deal vis-a-vis Gurkha recruitment pertains to the royalty that the British government has been paying to the Nepalese government. It has certainly not gone into Nepal's national treasury in the last 183 years that the Gurkhas have been in service with the British. While the royalty descends on mysterious hands, the poor Gurkhas continue to suffer, devoid of appreciation and resources to lead a decent life. ◆

Chapter Ninety-Three

Turning a Blind Eye

The Gurkhas of Nepal conjure up an image of total loyalty, bravery and honesty. Centuries of hard work, sacrifice and dedication have built these unique characteristics into them. The saga of young but poor highlanders who have crossed the seven seas as soldiers of fortune has caught the imagination of people throughout the world.

The British in India and the Nepalese fought a fierce battle in 1815 against each other but in the end both emerged as lasting friends. The Nepalese lost almost half its territory consequent to the Sugauli Treaty of 1816 but did not lose face. The British may have broken the Nepalese backbone in the battlefield but not before they realised that beating the Nepalese was no small achievement - it was tough. The British diplomacy paid off well when they made the Nepalese fight for and not against them ever since the Sugauli Treaty. This marked the beginning of the great Gurkha legend.

The most remarkable fight the Gurkhas fought on behalf of the British was in 1857 when the British imperial administration in India was faced with the problem of quelling the Indian mutiny. During the First World War, about 110,000 Gurkhas were recruited by the British. Of them, 20,000 were feared killed. In the Second World War, about 132,800 joined the British army and were engaged in historic battles in South-East Asia, the Middle East, Africa and Europe. During this war about 23,000 Gurkhas lost their lives. However, the Gurkhas bagged thirteen Victoria Crosses. The conferring of this highest award for valour meant so much to so many in Nepal.

When India became independent in 1947, the British Gurkhas were divided into two parts. Out of the ten Gurkha regiments stationed in India, four were taken to the Far East by the British while the remaining six regiments stayed with the Indian army. For ten years, about 15,000 British Gurkha soldiers were in action in what is now called Malaysia and Singapore quelling the communist guerrillas in particular. In 1962, the Sultan of Brunei was saved from being toppled in a violent coup by them. Since 1970, about 8,000 Gurkhas were stationed in Hong Kong as security forces. By the time of transfer of sovereignty to China in 1997, the strength of Gurkha troops in Hong Kong had been cut by half. It was in 1982 that the Gurkhas came in the global limelight again, during the British military operation in the Falklands. In the recent past, the Gurkhas were involved in the Gulf War and also in Bosnia-Herzegovina.

The UK-India-Nepal tripartite agreement still stands valid and under it the Nepalese boys continue to be, though in a reduced form, an integral part of the British regular army. But Gurkhas recruited by countries other than Britain and India are technically not covered by the Tripartite Agreement of 1947. The Nepalese government is too timid to take cognisance of this fact. There is a special contingent of over 900 Gurkhas in the Singapore police. The number is likely to go up. Brunei has maintained a Gurkha Reserve Unit comprising more that 2,200 security men. The government of Nepal pretends not to have noticed it, let alone take an appropriate action.

Besides these informal arrangements in which the Gurkhas are directly involved, there is a widespread demand for their services in several other countries. Informal consultations are on for recruitment of Gurkhas to bolster the Canadian and Australian armed forces. So far the Nepalese government has shown only a benign indifference to this international interest in the Gurkhas. If overtly the government suffers from a guilty conscience that it is letting its citizens defend and secure the interest of other countries, covertly the reason for inaction on the part of the Nepalese government may be traced to the fact that the ethnic groups that constitute the famous Gurkhas are still unrepresented at Nepal's decision-making level.

The Gurkha servicemen and ex-servicemen yield fairly high economic returns to Nepalese society directly at the rural grass-roots level. The remittance by the Gurkhas in foreign currency is an indirect benefit to the whole country. The enormity of the benefit can be gauged from the fact that the amount of annual pension to Gurkha ex-servicemen from India alone comes to about Rs. 6 billion. The Nepalese government is behaving like an ostrich as it ignores the likely economic impact of the on-going Gurkha recruitment, as well as high prospects of legitimate employment for others.

Where there are good prospects of honest deals and fair income for the people, the Nepalese government strangely turns a blind eye. But where there is the prospect for outright personal gain through shady deals, the enthusiasm on the government's part is unbelievably high-pitched.

◆

Chapter Ninety-Four

Disappearing Forest

Once upon a time, Nepal was famous for its lush green forests. The natives were proud of the greenery as being their wealth. The foreigners admired the Nepalese forests because they provided excellent hunting grounds. The British colonial bosses in India frequented the Nepalese jungles on elaborate safaris. Tigers, wild boars, deer and bears were the prime targets. It did not matter much in those days because wildlife was aplenty due to the fact that human encroachments were practically unknown, thanks to the malaria-bearing mosquitoes.

But the mosquitoes were gone as the Americans came. Indiscriminate application of DDT drove the mosquitoes out all right but marked the beginning of the slash and burn era. The forests were cleared for fresh human settlements. The process of legal and illegal felling of trees has not stopped since then. In no time the forest coverage lost its major part and was reduced to 20% from more than 60% of the country. It took only fifty years of 'modernisation'. The government claims forest coverage is 37% but that is, as many Nepalese know, only a figment of the imagination.

For more than three decades, the government vandalised the forests for national revenue. Every year it authorised clear felling in several hundred hectares of forest. The contractors armed with a permit to cut, say, 100 cubic feet of logs, would cut nothing less than 200 cubic feet by bribing the forest officials and guards in the area. Though the Nepalese, were the ones contracted to do the job, the Indian dealers often paid into the act. They profited more from forest destruction than the Nepalese, also because the logs were meant for use particularly as railway sleepers in India. Nepal has one of the best hardwoods, the *shorea robusta,* considered most ideal for railway tracks.

In one very typical episode, the King of Nepal gave a favourite sycophant of his a gift of the authority to cut 100,000 cubic feet of logs. The man had to pay Rs. 7 per cubic foot as a royalty to the government. He sold his right to an Indian contractor for Rs. 16 per cubic foot, straight away making a profit of Rs. 9 per cubic foot. But the actual market price for the same in India was Rs. 40. Imagine the eventual margin of profit for the Indian dealer. On top of that, the Indian dealer cut 300,000 cubic feet of logs based on the government permit which allowed only 100,000. The profit from this deal worked out like this: the government got Rs. 700,000, the Nepalese beneficiary received Rs. 900,000 whereas the Indian contractor amassed Rs. 12,000,000. In percentage terms, the government received 5%, the Nepalese contractor 6% and the Indian contractor 88%.

Whether it is the King's gift or the government's or local official's, tree felling invariably exceeds the specific range of the permit. So, rapid depletion of the forest wealth is inevitable. The deforestation in Nepal has been discussed all over the world and blamed for massive soil erosion and creation of a new island in the Bay of Bengal. Floods in Nepal, India and Bangladesh are also attributed to this phenomenon. If nothing else, the rising population of Nepal is heavily dependent on forest resources for firewood, fodder and timber for household use. The tragedy is that the massive amount of money spent on reforestation programmes have so far borne no fruit worth the name.

Finland came up with a million dollar plus purse ill the 1980s to help Nepal prepare an ambitious twenty-year master plan for the forestry sector. After an exercise spread over a number of years with international consultants in the vanguard, the project produced thirteen voluminous reports on ways and means to take care of Nepal's forest resources. None of the Nepalese forest officials ever read the reports except perhaps the executive summary. The reports are gathering dust in some corner. Some $1.7 billion, said the reports, was needed for forest development in Nepal. The idea never materialised. What actually materialised were luxurious apartments in Bangkok and Los Banos for two international consultants.

To retrieve the master plan Finland decided to invest more money. This time, it started what came to be known as institutional strengthening programme at phase 1, phase 2, and phase 3. The phases would have continued for infinity had Nepal not been gripped by a political upheaval in 1990. After what turned out to be a temporary halt, another great idea surfaced in the 'democratic' horizon of Nepal. Now the whole forest of Bara district about 32,430 hectares would be exploited for profit under a joint enterprise of the Nepalese and the Finnish investors.

According to the business plan, the Bara forest would be divided into 20 plots, one of which will be clear felled every year. After disposing of the logs and all vegetation, the cleared area would be reforested. What looks certain in the game is that a given plot will be stripped of the trees with no foolproof guarantee that it will be reforested the following year. The Finnish company is perfectly willing to accept the clear-felling responsibility but would have responsibility of reforestation taken by the Nepalese government because, as the Finn argued, it involves the risk of the cleared land being illegally grabbed leading to a law and order situation

Until April of 1998, the Nepalese government had not given a green signal to this project for fear of a public uproar. The Finnish government is tightening the screw of the Nepalese government, even threatened to withdraw other assistance from Nepal if the Finnish company interested in deforesting 32,430 hectares of land is not allowed to go ahead with the commercial project.

According to official estimates, a total of Rs. 8 billion can be raised from the sale of the Bara forest hardwood. After paying the royalty to the government and meeting other expenses, it is estimated that the entrepreneurs will save about Rs. 5 billion. The contract draft submitted by the Finnish company overrules all prohibitive clauses in Nepalese law regarding forests. In other words, once, the contract on the Bara forest is signed, the Finnish company will rule supreme over this valuable but dwindling resource of Nepal.

◆

Chapter Ninety-Five

You Can't, We Won't

Until 1950 Nepal had no modern roads. The people had to negotiate the distance, long or short, on foot. That was the only option, at least as far as north-south movement was concerned. In the case of east-west movement there was one option. One could enter India, use the Indian railways and then re-enter Nepal. A development-orientated government took over in 1951 and started building roads. However, the resources were extremely limited. By 1955, Nepal had about 600 km of roads. In forty years since, around 6,000 km have been added.

By far the most vital component of the road network in Nepal is the east-west highway that facilitates travel from one end of the country to another without going through India. The credit for conceptualising and launching this road goes undoubtedly to the late King Mahendra.

Local enthusiasm manifesting in terms of personal donation in cash or voluntary labour, though very encouraging, would not suffice. After some time international assistance started to flow. The Soviet Union, the Italians, the British, the Americans and the Indians offered to construct parts of the proposed highway. Some provided outright grants while others extended credit. The road presents a good view of variety of engineering techniques and sincerity on the part of the countries involved in the project. This perhaps is the best example of how a highway has to be built promptly. But the problem after four decades is the highway is still not complete. The reason? The east-west highway is clearly a victim of a dog in the manger mentality.

India was not happy with this road for political and economic reasons. But when so many countries agreed to help Nepal in this venture, India could not appear to be the odd man out. It showed interest in building a major part of the highway in the western sector. Nepal agreed but India started to drag its feet. Years rolled on but there was no sign of the promised construction coming up in that part. Exasperated by the Indian delay the Nepalese government decided to undertake construction on its own. About 75 km of road was roughly carved out but that was not good enough. Out of desperation, Nepal called for a World Bank loan and threw the project open to global bidding.

Among the bidders, China was chosen. It was just a matter of building about 200 km of road from Kohalpur to Mahakali, the westernmost portion of the east-west highway, through dense forests and innumerable rivers. Altogether twenty-three bridges were involved. The contract was signed and the work was to start shortly. Obviously the very thought of Chinese working so close to its border was unacceptable to the Indians. Pressure was mounted on Nepal to cancel the contract. India said it could not tolerate the presence of the hostile Chinese near its border. Armed with no political weapon to withstand the Indian pressure, Nepal quietly gave in. China was persuaded to forget the deal after a nominal compensation was paid which it gracefully accepted to save Nepal from embarrassment.

Had India taken the project in earnest the road would have been completed a long time ago. Hiring only a few labourers, India started the construction. An infrastructure of sorts was put up at the site but the instruction was 'go show'. It is still so. India has imposed a dog in the manger policy on this road. She neither built it nor allowed others to do so. But Nepal can do nothing because she has no power to pressurise a big country like India.

◆

Chapter Ninety-Six

The Bottleneck

Visit Nepal Year '98 was declared to attract half a million tourists during the year. Compared to other countries the projected figure is minuscule. But for Nepal, it is a big deal. Nepal has never received visitors in large numbers. The highest ever has not exceeded 350,000. In that sense, half a million visitors is not a tall order. What, after all, is the stumbling block? Why is the number of visitors to Nepal, a popular tourist destination, not increasing as indeed it should? Is it because there are insufficient hotel rooms or because Nepal has ceased to be a worthwhile tourist destination? Neither is true.

The problem lies in what appears to be an innocuous agreement between Nepal and India. The agreement allows a maximum of only 6,000 visitors from India by air in a week. This has nothing to do with constraint in air flights. The motive is to restrict the flow of visitors to Nepal. Until 1997, only 4,000 could fly in a week and it was only after the personal intervention of the prime minister of India that the number was raised to 6,000.

The restriction poses a big hurdle because most of the tourists from America, Europe and East Asia come to Nepal as an adjunct to their main visit to India. In their two-week holidays, they spend the major part of their time in India and hop to Nepal just for a day or two. Nepal benefits only marginally from those who visit her only as an extension of their Indian visit. But there are thousands who cannot even make a hop to Nepal because air seats are not available. There is no civilised justification for such a restriction but it has to be there in force because India wants it. Unless India wants it otherwise, Nepal's hands are tied.

As far as Nepal's beauty and hospitality are concerned, a million tourists a year need not have been a far-fetched dream. There are 632 hotels with more than 26,000 beds and their average occupancy rates is only 40% in Kathmandu and 26% in Pokhara, the second most important tourist destination. The supply far outweighs the demand which results in prices being low. The visitors may be saving money but the hotel industry is losing even a fair share of return on its investment. This is equally true with the number of travel agencies, trekking agencies and other ancillary services. The trekking service available at $80 per person two decades ago is being marketed for $20 at present. It is all because of cut-throat competition among a relatively large number of agencies for so few customers.

Tourism is a firm source of foreign exchange earning. Nepal earned $166 million in 1996, an increase from $50 million in 1980. But the average income from a tourist per day declined from $38 in 1980 to $32 in 1996. It is certainly not because tourists are spending less than before but because the lion's share of the benefit is going to the foreign travel agencies who are not averse to taking undue advantage of the internal contest among the Nepalese travel agents. The American, European and Japanese travel agencies charge their clients a standard global price but pay far less to their counterparts in developing countries. In that sense, only the crumbs are being picked up by Nepal's tourism industry. The big slice of the bread which is profusely buttered stays somewhere else.

◆

Chapter Ninety-Seven

The Burgeoning Burden

Foreign aid is unfortunately considered a panacea for all ills stemming from poverty and under-development. Nepal, being one of the poorest countries in the world, attracts international aid from all quarters and in all fields. During the Cold War when the world was divided into democratic and socialist camps, Nepal was perhaps one of the few exceptions, attracting assistance from both sides. Soviet and Chinese aid built new factories and roads while American, British, German, French and Indian assistance was spread over development of education, health, infrastructure, culture and so on.

Foreign aid has thus played a key role in Nepal's development over the last five decades. Just how pervasive foreign aid was can be judged from the fact that it covered more than 50% of Nepal's development budget. Annually the aid fluctuated between 40% to 60% of the total budget of Nepal, which is around $1 billion. The number of people who fear the Nepalese economy would collapse without foreign aid has not decreased a bit. Even those who are convinced of its rampant misuse dare not deride it completely. The ratio of foreign resources vis-a-vis indigenous resources would have to be examined to understand the upward trend in dependency syndrome. For three consecutive years - 1994 to 1997 - the ratio weighed heavily in favour of the former.

In terms of the actual volume though, foreign aid in Nepal is going down. Disbursement of foreign funds in Nepal was $476.2 million in 1994, $431.2 million in 1995 and $391.8 million in 1996. while it arguably is a reflection of donor fatigue, the gradual drop is equally attributable to the poor aid- absorptive capacity of Nepal.

Nepal has never been able to use more than 75% of the foreign resources at her disposal.

The proportion of loans is growing in relation to grants, causing an upswing in debt burden. In 1975, the grants constituted 75% of the foreign assistance but it declined to 34% in 1995. Over this twenty-year period, the volume of loans went up from 25% to 66% of the total external resources committed to Nepal.

This is further illustrated by the fact that bilateral assistance which often includes a grant aid is giving way to multilateral loans. In 1975, the bilateral sources provided 65% of the total foreign aid whereas in 1995, it has declined to 25%.

This has resulted in increase in the level of foreign debt. Nepal's net outstanding foreign loans in 1975 were Rs. 477.2 million ($9.5 million). It increased to the staggering figure of Rs. 128,044.4 million ($2.5 billion) in 1995. This is a 268 times increase in twenty years.

While outstanding foreign debts were equal to 40% of Nepal's total exports in 1975, the amount rose to 645% of its annual exports in 1995. This highlights that Nepal is in no position to pay its foreign debts from its export earnings.

Likewise, outstanding debts in relation to GDP increased from just 3% in 1975 to 54% in 1995. The total annual debt servicing increased from a mere Rs. 15 million ($0.3 million) in 1975 to Rs. 3,304 million ($66 million) in 1995.

It means that about one sixth of the foreign assistance goes back to the so-called donor countries themselves.

This overwhelming domination of foreign aid in the Nepalese economy notwithstanding, it would have been a matter of satisfaction had the aid been properly utilised to leave a positive imprint on the people's standard of living. But it has been officially established that foreign aid has by and large gone to waste owing to bureaucratic red tape, wrong technology, negligence and sheer incompetence of the international consultants. In addition, the resources have been siphoned off, over-invoiced, funnelled to questionable agencies and individuals, not to mention plunder perpetrated by the national as well as international decision makers.

The financial watchdogs of Nepal have come up with authentic proof of cases where millions of dollars have been misappropriated, misused and wasted. Unfortunately, most cases have gone unattended. Not a single person of consequence in

Nepal has ever been tried for corruption which everyone is aware is rampant from top to bottom. As a result, the country is buckling under the burden of foreign debts. The whole episode has generated a deep sense of anger and frustration in society. No wonder the foreign aid is no longer looked upon with much respect by the common folk who were said to be the main target beneficiaries of foreign aid in the first place.

◆

Epilogue

After hearing these harrowing tales, what else can one expect to see in Nepal except growing poverty? Common knowledge has it that Nepal is officially declared as one of the poorest countries on earth. About nine million out of the total 20 million citizens of Nepal live below the poverty line. The appalling thing is that the number of Nepalese poor is growing every year by 2.2%.

In 1977, the Planning Commission of Nepal discovered that 31.5% of the population in Nepal was in abject poverty. The central bank of Nepal said in a 1985 survey that the people below the poverty line had shot up to 43.1%. In 1991, the World Bank-UNDP survey concluded that the deprived in Nepal are 40% of the population. Many economists, however, claim that the situation is much worse than these studies have established.

The depth of poverty in Nepal is no less alarming. Nepal's GDP grew at the rate of 3.4% per annum over a period of twenty-five years between 1965 and 1990. In twenty-six years of tryst with economic development, per capita income registered an increase of only Rs. 301 ($5) whereas food consumption alone claims about 57% of total national expenditure. The monthly medical and education bill of one family is less than one dollar. Around 42% of total working time of Nepalese (of fifteen years of age and above) is expended on domestic chores like cooking, child care and cleaning. Another 15% of the time goes to what may be called subsistence activities - fuel and fodder collection, house repair and so on. The total assets of a farm family average at Rs. 39,000 ($780) with livestock accounting for about 75% of it. The total cash held by a rural family is less than 0.25% of total family assets.

The saving rate in Nepal is so low that it can hardly spur internal investment for development. The Nepalese consumed 90%

of the GDP in 1975 and 93.9% in 1990. This naturally brought domestic savings during this period down to 6.1% from 10%, hence the greater and greater role of extraneous resources in the development sector.

The economic condition of Nepal is dismal, and has to be viewed in the overall context of political, social and other variables. When national resources along with international funds are grossly misused for individual as opposed to broader public gains, the result cannot but be poverty of Himalayan proportions.

This is the natural consequence of the deplorable practice of managing national resources with mala fide intentions. The poor are doubly victimised, firstly by being marginalised by the stronger segments of society and secondly, by the seemingly interminable leakage of resources meant primarily for their welfare.

This is corroborated by a study that said half the people of Nepal have not been reached by state-sponsored development programmes. About 10% of the people have marginally benefited whereas only 5% have drawn full benefits from government programmes.

Fifty years of experiments in political, economic and social fields might have changed the quality of national infrastructure, popular aspirations and fundamental freedoms, but these achievements have gone in favour of a select few 10% or 20% of the population. The vast majority are still languishing in medieval backwardness.

The gap between the haves and have-nots is an accepted fact of life. A survey of the people's economic status has established that the top 20% of the population consume 45% of national produce and the bottom 50% of the people get only 26%. A similar study claims the share of income of the bottom 40% of the households during 1981-93 was 22%, while the top 10% had 27.7%. It is estimated that about 50% of households own only 7% of the land, working on holdings of less than half a hectare.

While on the one hand the majority of people suffer from hunger, illness, ignorance and joblessness, on the other hand the select few who wield political, economic and social power fiddle, with millions of rupees and, in most cases, millions of dollars. People expected to see changes in this state of affairs with the coming of democracy and individual freedom. The hopes have apparently been belied. Many believe the plundering of national resources today is more visible than ever before.

The unemployment situation has made life all the more difficult. The labour force increased at the rate of 183,000 per annum during the 1980s and 1990s, a rise of 2.9%. Between 1971-1991, the number of job seekers increased from 4,850,000 to 8,500,000. The National Planning Commission estimated that in 1992, there were 650,000 unemployed (7.6% of the total work force). How accurate the figures are is anybody's guess. Nepal has no system of registering the unemployed as the government provides no unemployment benefits to anyone. The guess is that the unemployment figure should be lot higher.

Poverty alleviation is nevertheless the primary objective of Nepal's economic planning, and all her development projects and so-called grass-roots programmes. But for all intents and purposes, Nepal has succeeded in poverty development rather than poverty alleviation. What is shocking is the conclusive observation of a research agency which said the structure of the Nepalese economy was neither conducive to sustained economic growth nor to the alleviation of poverty. It also predicts poverty perpetuation in Nepal.

Maybe it is poverty that has made the Nepalese susceptible to the very idea of getting rich overnight or someday. Nepal is now a wonderful land where smart fellows can easily sell dreams. The leaders in any discipline tend to succeed perhaps because they represent an opportunity for the common man to get rich or a dream of paradise not only for this life but also for life after death, as prescribed in religious scriptures. The cultural values based on the dominant Hindu and Buddhist ethos and traits treat all worldly miseries as preordained features of human life. Salvation lies not in mending this world but in getting rid of it for good by self-perpetuation and self- purification. It is perhaps because of this mindset that the Nepalese are swayed by improbable dreams of a better tomorrow, caring precious little for today.

Historically, the first vision of a rose garden came in the garb of democracy in the 1950s when most Nepalese did not even know how to write their own names. For a full decade the people were held in trance when they were told they had freedom of speech and freedom of organisation. It was at that time that a parliamentary constitution was framed followed by a general election based on universal suffrage. A political party came to power with a thumping majority. The then undisputed leader, B.P. Koirala, was a socialist by conviction and therefore close to Israel which had asserted itself as a separate entity in the troubled Middle East.

The Nepalese were abundantly fed with socialist dogmas and the great spirit of Israel. Indeed, the dreams of social benefits and securities were floated with gusto. Israel fascinated the Nepalese in no small measure. Fairy tales of bravery and nation-building were systematically disseminated. All those dreams were rudely torn apart when the parliamentary system in Nepal was abruptly abolished in the royal coup of 1960. With it the dream merchants went to high-security jails. One of the high-profile slogans in those years was that Nepal would be able to build anything from needles to aeroplanes within twenty years. Even after fifty years, Nepal imports both of them.

King Mahendra who took absolute control of state affairs in 1960 was no less a dreamer himself. He turned towards the East rather than the West for inspiration. Japan struck the royal chord. Nepal and Japan are both monarchies, and monarchies can produce miracles. If Japan was churning out one miracle after the other, why couldn't Nepal? The Nepalese did not realise that a price would have to be paid. The price was being loyal to the King, being obedient to the King and being respectful to the King. They abided by all the dictates of the state hoping to get catapulted to Japanese status. Needless to say, the dream remained unfulfilled. King Mahendra had taken them for a ride.

Then came the turn of his son, King Birendra, who embarked on a new dream of making Nepal a second Switzerland - neutral and peaceful. The Nepalese were promised Swiss prosperity along with zone of peace status for Nepal. When neither worked, they were promised the 'Asian standard'. But before he could play some more cards, more dreams to be precise, he lost absolute power in 1990.

The 1990s began with a Singapore obsession. The democratic leaders with a global view found in Singapore all that one can aspire for. 'We will make Nepal a Singapore,' was what the gullible Nepalese were made to listen to, preferably with rapt attention. When and how 'Singapore' would be realised did not matter to anybody, neither the speakers nor the audience because neither believed the dream would ever come true. All needed something to cling on to and the dream 'Singapore' was there. Even when grunting in darkness under not so infrequent loadshedding, the leaders mesmerised the people to think of shining Singapore and be illuminated within. They did it because that was the only light at the end of the long, dark tunnel.

When the Nepalese woke up from the long slumber induced by the hypnotic impact of the 'dream', they found their house in tatters. The people in Humla were starving to death, the Maoist guerrillas were dancing in their backyards and the girls were fleeing across the border to sell flesh for bread. While the youngsters were scrambling for jobs, the politicians had all gone in their sleek imported duty-free cars. The national television would rather flash the images of the famished women and children of Sudan. Or were they Nepalese? Before the Nepalese could be sure of their identities, they are airborne for Singapore, not knowing that the landing will be in Sudan. Flying surely a sweet dream, but landing a bitter reality. Who would know it better than the poor and helpless Nepalese?

There is a limit to tolerance. The patience of the people is wearing thin. Signs of the simmering anger of the poor are getting sharper and sharper with each passing day. A catastrophic cataclysm seems to be around the corner. There is no question that Nepal is heading towards a precipice of sorts. The inevitable has to come, not because the poor are born poor and should therefore remain poor, but because the poor have been made poorer by the sheer greed, folly and incompetence of those entrusted with the responsibility to shape and guide the destiny of the country.

◆

Bibliography

Agrawal, Nanda Kishore *Paper on Irrigation*, Nepal Water Resources Strategy Formulation, His Majesty's Government of Nepal, the World Bank, JGF Project, Kathmandu, April, 1997

Amatya, Dr Shaphalya, *Kingship and Nepalese Culture*, Kathmandu, 1997

Auditor General Report, Part I and Part II, Kathmandu, Auditor General Office, 1998

Bangdel, Lain S., *Stolen Images of Nepal*, Kathmandu

Birahi, Harihar, in *Bimarsha* (a vernacular weekly), Kathmandu, 10th April 1998

Briefing notes UNHCR, Kathmandu, 1997,1998

Children and Women of Nepal. A Situation Analysis, Kathmandu, UNICEF Nepal, 1996

Commission of Investigation on Abuse of Authority, Annual Reports, Kathmandu, 1995,1996,1997,1998

Devkota, Grishman Bahadur, *Nepal ko Rajanaitic Darpan* Parts I and II, Kathmandu, Upendra Bhadur Devkota, 1983

Dixit, Kanak Mani, 'Foreign aid in Nepal: No bang for the buck', in *Everest Herald*, Kathmandu, 25th November 1997

The Eighth Plan, Nepal Planning Commission, Kathmandu, 1992-97

Gewali, Hemraj, in *Kantipur* (a vernacular daily), Kathmandu, 15th November 1997, 19th March 1998

Curung, Maj. Dipak Bahadur, 'Pension Increase of British Gurkhas', in *Ex-servicemen Message*, special issue, First national convention, Kathmandu, 1997

Gurung, Padam Bahadur, President, Nepal Ex-servicemen Association., *Four-point Demand to the British Government*, Why?, Kathmandu, 1997

Gyawali, Hem Raj, *The Kathmandu Post*, (an English daily), Kathmandu, March 28 1998

Hakahaki, Kathmandu, Center for Development Communication (CDC) February 1998

Hillel, Dr Daniel, Professor Emeritus, University of Massachusetts, *Paper on Phase I Consolidated Draft Report*, Nepal Water Resources Strategy Formulation, His Majesty's Government of Nepal, the World Bank, JGF Project, Kathmandu, January 1997

Himal, Himal Association, Kathmandu, July/August 1995, July 1998

Khadka, Narayan, *Foreign Aid and Foreign Policy, Major Powers and Nepal*, Kathmandu

Khanal, Dhundi Raj, *The Rising Nepal*, (English daily), Kathmandu, 28th May 1998

Kshatri, Rajendra Kishore, *Paper on Legal and International Issues*, Nepal Water Resources Strategy Formulation, His Majesty's Government of Nepal, the World Bank, JGF project, Kathmandu, April 1997

Master Plan for Forestry Sector, Kathmandu, His Majesty's Government of Nepal, Ministry of Forestry, 1988

Nepal Ex-servicemen Association, *Memorandum to Prime Minister of Nepal*, Kathmandu, July 1996

Nepal Human Development Report, Nepal South Asia Center, Kathmandu, 1998

Pande, Sriram Raj, *A Study of Foreign Assistance in Nepal*, New Era, Kathmandu, November 1997

Pradhan, Bhubanesh Kumar, *Paper on Nepal Water Resources*, Nepal Water Resources Strategy Formulation, His Majesty's Government of Nepal, the World Bank, JGF Project, Kathmandu, April, 1997

Prakashan, Aastha, in *Jana Astha* (a vernacular weekly), Kathmandu, 18th March 1998

Prakashan, Prativadha, *Kathmandu Today* (a vernacular monthly), Kathmandu, 14th January 1998, 13th February 1998, 28th April 1998

Reports on Irrigation Development in Retrospect: Search for a Breakthrough, Vol. 1, Main Report and Vol. 2. Annexes, National Planning Commission, Kathmandu, September 1994

Report of Commission on Inventory of Public Land in Kathmandu, HMG, Ministry of Land Reform, Kathmandu, 1995

Reports of Public Accounts Committee, House of Representatives, Parliament House, Kathmandu, Fourth report 1995, Fifth report, Parts I and II, 1996

Report on Godavari Marble Factory and its Impact on Environment, Ministry of Forest and Soil Conservation, Kathmandu, 1991

Rimal, Madhav Kumar, *Spotlight* (an English weekly), Kathmandu, March 1998

Sharma, Ujol, *HImalaya Times* (a vernacular daily), Kathmandu, (Magh 28, 2052) March 1995

Shrestha, Hari Om, *Paper on Hydropower,* Nepal Water Resources Strategy Formulation, His Majesty's Government of Nepal, the World Bank, JGF Project, Kathmandu, April 1997

Shrestha, Keshab Lal *Mahakali Sandhi ra Rashtriya Heet ko Sawal,* Kathmandu, 1997

Shrestha, Shambhu, *Dristi* (a vernacular weekly), Kathmandu, 24th March 1998

Shrestha, Subas, *Mulyankan* (a vernacular monthly), Kathmandu, (Mangsir, 2054) 1997

Suruchi, Kathmandu, (Falgun 3,2049), March 1992,

Treaty between His Majesty's Government and the Government Of India Concerning the Integrated Development of the Mahakali River including Sarada Barrage, Tanakpur Barrage and Pancheshor Project, Kathmandu, 1996

Thapa, Bandhu *Deshantar,* (a vernacular weekly), Kathmandu, 2nd June 1991, 18th September 1991, 30th May 1993, 18th August 1993, 19th January 1997, 16th February 1997, 16th March 1997, 27th April 1997, 18th May 1997, 11th June 1997, 3rd August 1997, 19th October 1997, March 1998, 17th May 1998

Vaidya, Nirjara Nanda, *Paper on Hydrology,* Nepal Water Resources Strategy Formulation, His Majesty's Government of Nepal, the World Bank, JGF Project, Kathmandu, April 1997

◆